VANISHED!

VANISHED!

Mysterious Disappearances

DAVID CLARK

MICHAEL O'MARA BOOKS LIMITED

First published in 1990 by
Michael O'Mara Books Ltd
9 Lion Yard
Tremadoc Road
London SW4 7NQ

Reprinted 1991

A CIP catalogue record for this book is available
from the British Library

ISBN 1-85479-023-4

Designed by Martin Bristow
Picture research by Marion Pullen

Typeset by Florencetype Ltd, Kewstoke, Avon
Printed and bound by Richard Clay, Bungay, Suffolk

CONTENTS

Contents

ACKNOWLEDGMENTS

The Publishers gratefully acknowledge permission to reproduce the pictures on the following pages:

Associated Press/Topham: between pp. 96–7 top left

Compix, New York: opposite p. 96; opposite p. 97

The Hulton-Deutsch Collection: between pp. 32–3 below right; between pp. 64–5 right; opposite p. 129 below

The Illustrated London News Picture Library: opposite p. 32 below

The Mansell Collection: opposite p. 65 below; opposite p. 128 below

Peter Newark's Western Americana: between pp. 32–3 above right; opposite p. 65 above

Popperfoto: between pp. 32–3 left; between pp. 64–5 left; between pp. 96–7 right

Syndication International: opposite p. 32 above; opposite p. 64; between pp. 128–9 left

Times Newspapers: between pp. 128–9 right

Topham Picture Library: opposite p. 33; between pp. 96–7 left below; opposite p. 128 above; opposite p. 129 above

INTRODUCTION

Each year, in Britain alone, around 25,000 people 'disappear'. All save 10 per cent are found. But what has happened to the two and a half thousand human beings who are not located? Have they simply vanished 'into thin air'? The total number involved is disturbing enough, but when multiplied on a global scale the problem can be seen as one of truly horrendous proportions. If, then, the issue is so serious, it is reasonable to ask why officialdom prefers to do little about it. As with UFO phenomena it is sometimes easier to ignore the existence of something we do not understand than to investigate the possible reality of events which demonstrate our pitiful, primeval understanding of the Universe.

One of the earliest stories of an inexplicable disappearance which I remember having recounted to me concerned a merchant seaman who decided to climb an abandoned lighthouse. It must have occurred in those far-off days of the high-masted clippers, when sailors had to climb for a living and actually enjoyed doing it. The seaman was accompanied by a friend, and together they made their way gingerly up the decaying stone staircase which might, at any moment, crumble away beneath them.

Due in large measure to their seafaring skills, they reached the top safely and, leaning over the parapet surrounding the beacon-housing, began to wave and shout in an effort to attract the attention of their companions below. Under the strain of this unaccustomed activity, part of the parapet gave way, and the seaman whose idea it had been to scale the edifice, plunged to the ground.

His companion leapt down the winding staircase, throwing all caution to the winds in his panic. When he reached the bottom, however, and emerged into the daylight, he was amazed to see his friends chatting idly as though nothing had happened. In fact, nothing *had* happened for no one had seen or heard the unfortunate man fall. Despite an intensive search of the light-house, the surrounding land and the water, no trace of him was ever found. At some point between the parapet and the ground, he had vanished. . . .

A sketchy outline of a very similar story also comes to mind. It involves the old motor-racing circuit at Brooklands, near Weybridge in Surrey, Britain's premier venue for the sport from its inception in 1907 to the Second World War. Although later much missed by enthusiasts, the track had acquired a reputation as something of a death-trap so the move to the wartime airfield at Silverstone was welcomed by many. Great names in British racing, such as Hancock, Campbell, Segrave and Lambert, pepper the story of Brooklands, and it was shortly before the death of Percy Lambert that the following strange event occurred. This places it at some time during, or shortly before, 1913.

Percy Lambert crashed while making an attempt on the Brooklands lap record. He disappeared behind the famous Members' hill but did not re-appear at the other side, having burst a tyre on the bend and suffering a fractured skull in the subsequent crash. A colleague of Lambert's, during the course of a short handicap race over the outer circuit of the track, also turned into the Members' hill bend and failed to re-appear. Unlike Lambert, however, he had not crashed. Quite simply, he went into the bend and literally disappeared 'around the corner'. No trace of driver or vehicle was ever found.

Many years after first hearing this story, I met a man who claimed to have seen the apparition of a driver in goggles and a leather helmet on the Brooklands circuit itself. This ghost is believed by some to be that of Percy Lambert, and by others to be that of Vincent Herman, the first driver to be killed on the track during the first season of competition. But could it, I wondered, be the driver who disappeared, encased in a sort of time-capsule, condemned for eternity to race around and around the cambered cement-white surface?

These are just two examples from what is an inexhaustible reservoir of stories of mysterious disappearances: stories of vanishings by land, sea and air which defy explanation. The world of mysterious disappearances is a fascinating one. This book contains many of the best known and some of the least known. We study them today as impartial observers. It is quite likely, however, that some of us will ourselves constitute the subject matter for additional chapters.

1

INTO THE UNKNOWN

Colonel Percy Fawcett

In 1927 a French civil engineer, Roger Courteville, was passing through the state of Minas Gerais in Brazil when he came upon a white man, about 60 years of age, with long, grey hair and an unkempt beard. He wore a khaki shirt and trousers and a bush hat. Courteville found him sitting on the roadside, apparently exhausted, his legs covered with mosquitoes. 'I say,' said Courteville in English, 'the mosquitoes seem to take care of you.' The man looked up quizically and replied, with great stoicism, 'Those poor animals are hungry too.' Courteville concluded his account of this strange meeting (later published in the *Journal* of the Royal Geographical Society) with the comment: 'We went on our way, leaving the poor man calmly watching the mosquitoes devouring his legs.' The story caused a sensation when it reached Britain because it was widely believed that the poor old man in question was none other than Colonel Percy Fawcett, who had mounted an expedition into darkest Brazil two years before and from whom nothing had been heard since.

In the present day and age, when voyages to the Moon are so commonplace as to be hardly worth making any more, it is difficult for us to appreciate the level of excitement generated by exploration of the heartlands of the world's continents. When Fawcett began his trek into the Brazilian interior, the South Pole had been conquered only 15 years before, Mount Everest would remain unconquered for another quarter of a century, and air travel was in its infancy. Fawcett was heading for the great unknown, in much the same way as a manned spacecraft today might head for Mars.

The Colonel left it rather late in life to begin his great adventure, although at 57 years of age he was still hale and hearty, with the physical strength and constitution of many men half his age. And he had always harboured a wandering instinct. As a young officer in Sri Lanka he had spent much of his spare time exploring the heavily forested interior, guided by rumours, maps and legends concerning ruins of ancient cities and buried treasure. Yet, until now, his quarry had always eluded him. Approaching the twilight of his life, he now made a bid for the biggest prize of all: El Dorado.

The story of El Dorado is as teasing and as enigmatic as the story of Fawcett himself. The legend took root in the heady times of the Spanish conquistadors, in the sixteenth century, with the brutal conquest of the Inca Empire of Peru by Pizarro. The fabulous wealth of the Incas gave rise to stories of still greater riches hidden beyond the Andes, and of a civilization of such splendour that the king himself was rumoured to be painted in gold – El Dorado, the 'gilded man'.

Fawcett gleaned much of his knowledge of this fabled kingdom from documents held in the National Library of Rio de Janeiro, according to which seemingly inexhaustible mines of gold, silver and diamonds had been discovered by itinerant Portuguese in central Brazil in the early seventeenth century. An actual city, deserted but still showing traces of fabulous wealth, was located, again by the Portuguese, a century later. But no record remained of the exact location of either mines or city.

The Colonel made an abortive attempt to solve the riddle with an expedition in 1920 and, although a failure, some valuable lessons were learned. 'Success,' he wrote, 'depends on the selection of limited personnel, able if need be, to do without transport under extremely trying conditions.' And conditions were indeed 'trying', with blood-sucking bats, deadly snakes, hideous poisonous spiders, swamps and hostile natives all to be encountered.

The second, and final, expedition set out from Cuyaba into the interior on 20 April 1925. It consisted of the 'limited personnel' of Fawcett himself, his son Jack, and Jack's friend Raleigh Rimmell. Within a month they reached Baccairi, near the source of the River Verde, from where they journeyed to the last resting place of Fawcett's first expedition, named by him as 'Dead Horse

Camp'. From here Fawcett wrote a letter dated 29 May 1925 in which he said, 'We can bathe ourselves here, but insects make it a matter of great haste. Nevertheless, the season is good. It is very cold at night and fresh in the morning; but the insects and heat come by midday, and from then on until six o'clock in the evening it is sheer misery in camp.' He went on: 'My calculations anticipate contact with the Indians in about a week or ten days. Our two guides are more and more nervous as we push farther into Indian country. I shall continue to prepare dispatches from time to time, in hopes of being able to get them out eventually through some tribe of Indians.'

But no more dispatches did get out. This in itself was not a cause for immediate concern, because Fawcett had anticipated being enveloped in the jungle for at least two years. Roger Courteville's story surfaced at the end of this two year period – that is to say, when news of the expedition was to be expected. The year 1927 was not a particularly newsworthy one and the press, desperately on the lookout for good copy, pitched into it with a hearty appetite. And so began the long search for the Colonel and his companions.

In May 1928 the first rescue party was organized. It was led by Commander George Dyott. In contrast to Fawcett's practice of travelling light, Dyott insisted on a party which included 20 native bearers, 64 bullocks, 10 mules and a great deal of audio-visual equipment. From Dead Horse Camp, Dyott struck out for the River Kuliseu and managed to make contact with some Anauqa Indians, one of whom wore around his neck a medallion which, on closer scrutiny, was found to be a brass label stamped with the name of the City firm which had furnished Fawcett with his supplies.

The Indians swore that this had been a present from the Colonel. After Fawcett had left them, they said, his campfire smoke had been sighted rising above the trees, farther and farther away, for five days afterwards. On the sixth day there was no smoke, and the Anauqa chief was of the opinion that the small party had been massacred by the neighbouring Suya tribesmen. Dyott, however, suspected the Anauqa themselves of the deed, especially as the Anauqa chief Aloique appeared to be wearing a pair of Fawcett's trousers. But Dyott did not have long to ponder on the possibility at the time. Following a warm welcome, prompted perhaps by curiosity, the party found the Anauqa becoming more restless, with constant demands for presents. It was only by exercising stealth that Dyott was able to escape during the hours of darkness, thus narrowly avoiding the fate of compounding the mystery he had set out to solve.

As late as 1932, sightings of Fawcett were still occurring. For example, in that year a Swiss hunter named Stephan Rattin arrived at the British Consulate in São Paulo claiming that he had discovered Fawcett. While hunting in the Mato Grosso near Tapajos he had entered a native village where he encountered a white man being held prisoner. Clad in nothing but skins, the prisoner identified himself as a British colonel, begging Rattin to seek out a Major Paget who would come to his rescue as soon as he heard of his pitiful condition. He showed Rattin a ring, the description of which enabled Mrs Fawcett to identify it as the one her husband always wore. Interestingly enough, Fawcett had also known a Major Paget, who had helped to finance his expedition. Armed with this apparent confirmation, Stephan Rattin returned to the jungle to effect the Colonel's rescue – and was never heard of again.

Over the succeeding years 'reliable' reports of Fawcett's fate came to light with enough regularity to keep public interest alive. In 1933 the leader of an expedition to the Kuluene River, Virginio Pessione, reported that three white men, whose descriptions fitted those of the Fawcett party, had been living for some years with the Aruvudu Indians. The youngest (Jack Fawcett) had married an Indian woman who had borne him a white, blue-eyed son. In 1934 two American missionaries, Guiley and Halverson, told a very similar story – only in their version the Kirikuru Indians were the adopted tribe. In 1935 two brothers, Patrick and Gordon Ulyatt, made two expeditions to the Mato Grosso in the course of which they ascertained that the local rubber gatherers claimed to know much about Colonel Fawcett.

The most celebrated of the later expeditions was led by a journalist, Edmar Morel, in 1943. Morel hoped to locate Jack Fawcett's alleged son and, in the course of his search, met with Izariri, the Kalapos chief, who apparently admitted to killing all three white men. Morel also succeeded in finding a boy called Dulipe, whom he believed to be the much talked of white child, and took him to São Paulo. The wretched Dulipe, however, turned out to be a native albino, the condition of albinism being not unknown among local tribes.

Colonel Fawcett's younger son, Brian, who himself lived and worked in Peru for many years, continued to search for the answer to his father's disappearance, but by 1953, when he edited an edition of the Colonel's memoirs, it seemed that even he had given up all hope. Fresh interest was aroused on the book's publication for even then it seemed possible that Fawcett could still be alive, a demented old man, attired in rags, wandering aimlessly through the jungles of the Mato Grosso, ever waiting for the rescue that one day might still come. Ten years later, when the clearance of the tropical rain forests was under way, it was thought that the process might somehow throw up clues to Fawcett's ultimate fate; but it never did, only succeeding for all time in obliterating any lingering hopes.

So what did actually befall the 1925 Fawcett expedition? The most likely explanation is that, weakened by disease, the party was finished off by natives, the most likely culprits being the Anauqa, although it could just as well have been any one of a handful of mutually hostile tribes. As Dyott's substantial party was in considerable danger, Fawcett's compact and comparatively defenceless group would have made easy pickings. Or, having failed in his search for El Dorado, had Fawcett hidden himself in the jungle, too ashamed to tell the world of his failure? Or had he, as some said, 'gone native', settling down among the Indians as a much-venerated great white chief? Or had he, after all, found the fabled city, which had turned out to be a counterpart of Shangri-La, a fantastic world of eternal youth?

If no solution could be found in the land of the living, perhaps something could be gleaned from beyond the grave? Just as today leading clairvoyants, upon the demise of a prominent personality, clamour to tell the world of messages received, so in the 1930s no medium worth his or her salt could afford to ignore the possibilities offered by the disappearing Colonel. One of the most intriguing responses came from the society clairvoyant Mrs St John Montague. Staring piercingly into her crystal ball, Mrs St John Montague perceived three men:

> One lay on the ground, his head resting on his arm. His clothes were in ribbons. He did not stir, and appeared to be dead. Near by,

17

hacking a way through the undergrowth with an axe, was another man. With his arms he supported a young companion. Both were in rags, with long hair and beards. They were gaunt and starved-looking. Both wore wisps of blood-stained bandages, and the younger of the two seemed to be at the point of death.

According to Mrs Montague, the crystal then showed the crouching forms of naked savages armed with blowpipes and spears. The crystal swam with blood and, when it cleared, it showed the lifeless forms of the three white men being borne away.

Another, more celebrated medium, Geraldine Cummins, claimed to have made direct contact with the departed spirit of Fawcett, according to which the expedition had succeeded in finding the lost city which, it transpired, had proved to be an outpost of the mythical civilization of Atlantis. And Jack Fawcett had indeed married an Indian girl, before both he and Raleigh Rimmell had been killed on the orders of an ostensibly friendly Indian chief. The Colonel's own death, at a later date, had also been a violent one. Whatever the truth of the matter, further than beyond the grave one cannot go. . . .

Raymond Maufrais

Colonel Fawcett's disappearance captured the public imagination and commanded attention on a worldwide scale for more than 30 years. Yet there are others who have been swallowed up in the vastness of the South American jungles and whose disappearances have gone relatively unnoticed – as in the case of the Frenchman, Raymond Maufrais.

At the time of his disappearance in 1950 at the age of 23, Maufrais was a seasoned explorer, having undertaken much exploration in the Mato Grosso. Although he travelled alone he knew the jungle, its dangers and how to deal with them. Having survived the menace of the Mato Grosso, which had defeated Fawcett 25 years before, Maufrais finally succumbed to the rigours of French Guiana, from where he had set out with the intention of crossing the Tumuc-Humac mountains and making his way through unexplored territory to the Amazon.

Raymond's father, Edgar, first learned of his son's disappearance in a newspaper report of July 1950, which spoke of Raymond's abandoned kit on the banks of the River Tampuri in French Guiana – and of the belief that he had been the victim of Oyaricoulet Indians. Edgar Maufrais beggared himself in undertaking mission after mission to search for his son, convinced that he must still be alive, held captive by a tribe of Indians.

During the course of his searches, Edgar Maufrais did encounter several white men. One of these was a Mr Grings, described as 'thin, emaciated and stripped to the waist', with 'a white goatee beard and probably around sixty'. Grings was an American Salvation Army missionary who carried a portable record player and a collection of records in an Indian dialect which told the story of the gospels.

Edgar Maufrais' first expedition, in 1952, ended with the loss of most of his equipment and all of his money in a boating accident on the River Maroni's Cotica Rapids. Although in some respects a success – he had travelled from the Amazon to French Guiana across the Tumuc-Humacs – he had failed to achieve his objective, to find his son.

For his second expedition a year later, Maufrais aimed to follow the Amazon to Alenquer and then to turn inland to Bom

Futuro where, it was alleged, a white man fitting Raymond's description had been seen, but this attempt met with little better luck than the first. Reliable guides were hard to come by and funds for equipment and necessary expenses were low.

Many more expeditions followed, during the course of which Maufrais managed to ascertain that, in January 1950, Raymond had set out from Degrad Claude to float down the River Tamouri by raft to Bienvenue. When his raft broke up on the rocks, Raymond, wearing only shorts and with a small bag containing a knife, compass, notebook, pencil and matches, made an ill-advised attempt to reach Bienvenue by swimming. But he had not allowed for the rapids on the Tamouri and, to avoid them, he had been forced to make a detour on foot through the jungle. It was this decision that proved his undoing. Unable to return upstream because of the current, he was thrown on the mercy of the jungle, teeming with scorpions, poisonous spiders and vampire bats. In the vicinity of his son's last known campsite Edgar Maufrais found a rusty, headless screwdriver and a small saucepan without a handle: scant reward for all his efforts.

Edgar remained convinced that his son was still alive. He believed, despite all the evidence to the contrary, that Raymond had survived, battling through the worst of his ordeal to be taken captive and held prisoner by an unspecified band of semi-nomadic tribesmen. Indeed, from time to time there would come to light vague stories of a white man living forcibly among Indians deep within the interior.

In response to one such tale Edgar planned an expedition into Dutch Guiana. Before he started out it became apparent that the story was a hoax. The perpetrator had hoped to profit by acting as a paid guide to Maufrais. It speaks much for his growing state of desperation at this time that, despite uncovering the plot, Maufrais still decided to explore the region. He carried with him photographs of Raymond, which he would press on passing natives in the hope that they would recognize the likeness. Edgar was the first white man many of them had ever seen; the sight of a white man of any description would have etched itself deeply on their memories. Edgar even took to carving his name on tree trunks in case Raymond happened by. The heroic search had become a magnificent obsession. Edgar Maufrais never found his missing son.

Mallory and Irvine

It is a truism that success in exploration does not necessarily guarantee fame. The most successful Amazonian explorer of all time was a New Yorker, Dr Hamilton Rice, who over a period of 20 years undertook a series of geographical-cum-anthropological-cum-medical explorations into the interior. His 1908 expedition led to the famous newspaper denial: 'Explorer Rice denies he was eaten by cannibals.' The zenith of Hamilton Rice's career came in 1924, when he set off to discover whether the headwaters of the River Uraricoera joined up with the Orinoco. His quest involved a journey of a thousand miles across some of the most inhospitable terrain in the world. Yet today, Hamilton Rice is forgotten. Edgar Maufrais' twelfth expedition alone involved negotiating 500 miles of impossible terrain – and it must be remembered that he was a man of limited experience and even more limited means. He too is a neglected figure. The name of Fawcett, however, associated as it is with the concept of heroic failure, lives on.

In much the same way, the names of Scott and Franklin spring to mind before that of Amundsen in the realms of polar exploration. And sharing the glory of Hillary and Tensing, conquerors of Everest, are two who tried and failed nearly 30 years before: George Mallory and Andrew Irvine. As Fawcett was in the act of disappearing in the Brazilian jungle, so their own tragedy was taking place thousands of miles away on the other side of the world in a very different environment.

Climbing to a height of 29,000 feet presents a demanding challenge. To the Tibetan Buddhists, Mount Everest was a vengeful goddess intent on destroying her assailants. Piercing winds and biting cold were part of her outer defences. Treacherous precipices and ice-falls, with the ever-present danger of avalanches, the fearful violence of which could fling a man against bare ice with such force as to shatter his body and skull like an egg-shell – such were the mountain's second line of defence. If all these obstacles were overcome, and if the climbers escaped the dual ravages of frostbite and snow-blindness, there would come the most difficult hurdle of all: the problems attendant upon ascending into an incredibly thin atmosphere.

The process of breathing could become an experience of acute agony with each laboured inhalation. Without an adequate oxygen intake a person could become intensely irritable, losing all sense of time, place and responsibility – far more serious than the physical symptoms.

For what proved to be his final attempt on the summit in the spring of 1924, there were those who criticized Mallory for taking as his partner the youthful Irvine, when much more experienced men than the 22-year-old undergraduate were available. Other members of the expedition included Colonel E. F. Norton, a serving Indian Army man and alpine climber; Dr Howard Somervell, a London surgeon who eventually devoted himself to the care of a medical mission in India; and Neil Odell, a geologist whose fitness surpassed that of Mallory himself. As it was, Odell was left to bring up the rear and was destined to play an important supporting role.

As with polar exploration the assault was to be channelled through a series of prepared camps, from Camp I at 16,800 feet through to Camp VI at 26,800 feet, which would serve as a final base for the remaining 2,200 feet to be tackled.

On 6 June, Mallory and Irvine were climbing between Camps IV and V. On the 7th they ascended to Camp VI, established by Norton and Somervell three days earlier. The morning of the 8th was cloudy, with sleet and snow rendering visibility very poor. At about 1pm the atmosphere suddenly cleared. Odell, who had reached Camp V at 25,200 feet, scanned the summit ridge and final peak. Then, dramatically, his attention became riveted on a tiny black spot on the ridge. A second black spot appeared and moved up to join the first. Both moved on together, but as quickly as the cloud had cleared it fell once more, obscuring the distant figures. Mallory and Irvine were never seen again.

From their position Odell judged that they were well behind schedule. That they had encountered bad conditions and unforeseen obstacles was certain. Odell waited, but the mist now seemed immovable, so he pushed on up to Camp VI, which he reached by 2pm. The weather had deteriorated to such an extent that he was sure the pair must have had to turn back and were on their way down. He continued to wait until late afternoon, but no one came and he had no alternative but to return to Camp IV.

Next day, displaying great courage and determination, he returned to Camp VI – to find nothing. Following a courageous but futile search, he finally had to admit that Mallory and Irvine were not coming back.

Nine years passed before another British expedition was permitted to enter Tibet for an attempt on Everest. This 1933 expedition also failed in its objective, but it did turn up one interesting item: an ice-axe identified as belonging to either Mallory or Irvine, discovered at 28,000 feet. Its bright steel head was unrusted and its shaft was in perfect condition.

Two mysteries remained, and still remain, to be solved. In the first place, did they actually reach the peak of Mount Everest, 30 years before Hillary and Tenzing? Odell always believed they did. And if they did attain the peak, what happened to them afterwards? Do their bodies lie buried deep in the snow, encased in sub-zero tombs of ice, fully preserved and awaiting discovery? A sinister element was introduced into the story when rumours began to circulate about a third figure having been seen alongside those of the two climbers on that afternoon of 8 June 1924. If true, then who or what was it? This, in turn, led to speculation about the Yeti or so-called Abominable Snowman, and not all of it can be dismissed as nonsense.

It has been presumed that the two men fell to their deaths, but all variations on such an explanation are dependent upon Mallory, a mountaineer of 20 years' experience and veteran of three Everest expeditions, making a simple slip or error of judgement. Is it likely that he would? As Sherlock Holmes once remarked, when the impossible has been excluded, whatever remains, however improbable, must be the truth. So is it conceivable that the Abominable Snowman had, by startling the climbers, sent them hurtling to their deaths?

It is difficult to dismiss the Yeti as a creature of pure invention. The first Everest reconnaissance expedition in 1921 reported seeing a number of dark specks moving in the distance against the backcloth of the driven snow in the Lhapta-La Pass, while, at an altitude of 20,000 feet, human-like footprints were encountered. Indeed, the history of Everest expeditions is peppered with sightings of strange footprints by such eminent mountaineers as John Hunt, Edmund Hillary and Eric Shipton. Shipton's famous photographs showing a track of huge, unidentifiable footprints remain the most convincing evidence for the creature's existence.

Taken in 1951 during Shipton's own reconnaissance expedition, they were discovered on the Menlung Glacier near the Nepal-Tibet border at 18,000 feet and continued for almost a mile along the glacier's edge. The indentations were 18 inches long and 13 inches wide and suggested a creature with three small toes and a large rounded one. In 1978 John Hunt photographed a similar set of tracks.

It has been suggested that the Yeti is a surviving form of Neanderthal man who lived 40,000 to 100,000 years ago. Perhaps a few Neanderthals, driven to the most inhospitable corners of the earth, survived and, unmolested in the wilderness, continued to breed. In recent years much anthropological evidence tending to confirm that this is the case has come to light. A close encounter with such a creature would be cause enough for the most experienced mountaineer to panic. Without such a theory the disappearance of Mallory and Irvine must remain one of the world's most impenetrable mysteries.

2

DISAPPEARING 'DIPLOMATS'

Benjamin Bathurst

The disappearance of Benjamin Bathurst at Perleberg, near Berlin, in 1809 must surely rank as one of the strangest on record – the more so as, for reasons which will become apparent, it was thoroughly investigated and well documented at the time.

Bathurst was, as they say, well-born, being the third son of a bishop. The eldest brother became Archdeacon of Norwich and the second eldest was aide to Wellington during the Peninsular Campaign of 1808–14. Benjamin became a diplomat. His domestic circumstances were less than fortunate, his only son being thrown by a horse and killed, and a daughter drowning in the Tiber. He himself was to be lost without trace in the murky waters of international espionage.

Early in 1809 he was sent to Vienna by his kinsman Earl Bathurst, Secretary of State for the Foreign Office. His mission was a secret one to the court of the Emperor Francis at a time of critical importance in the Napoleonic Wars. At the Battle of Austerlitz in 1805, Napoleon had smashed the Russian and Austrian armies and Austria had since been a neutral observer of European hostilities. Unofficially she had been building up a new army of 300,000 men, a manoeuvre which Britain was happy to encourage. Bathurst did his best to persuade the Austrians that his political masters were about to initiate a major new offensive against the French emperor and that Austrian support would be an essential ingredient of the plan. The Austrians complied and mobilized.

As a result of his successful persuasion, Bathurst came to believe that Napoleon bore him a considerable degree of malice and was, moreover, intent on personal revenge. Certainly, his position at the Austrian court became a little fragile after the Austrians' sound drubbing at Wagram on 6 July 1809, and in the autumn of that year he set out on his journey home. His fears for his own safety can be well understood, for he was compelled to travel through a Europe dominated in its entirety by the enemies of Britain. There was some initial difficulty, therefore, in deciding upon a safe route. He rejected the seaborne route via Trieste and Malta – an odd decision since, after Trafalgar four years previously, Britain had control of the high seas. Instead he decided on the overland passage through north Germany via Berlin. Accompanying him was his private secretary.

Travelling as a merchant under the assumed name of Koch, he arrived at Perleberg, midway between Berlin and Hamburg, at about noon on 25 November. His carriage drew to a halt at the post-house and, while horses were being changed, he ordered some refreshment at the White Swan Inn nearby. Upon finishing his meal he made a point of visiting the local garrison and sought an interview with the commander, Captain Klitzing, informing him that he feared for his life and requesting protection at the inn. Two soldiers remained with him there until seven o' clock, when he dismissed them and ordered the horses to be made ready by nine. Travelling by night, he thought, would be safer than travelling by day.

He stood outside the inn, watching his luggage being replaced in the carriage, stepped round to the heads of the horses – and was never seen again. Inexplicably, without a word, a cry, an alarm of any sort, he was gone – spirited away. All the while attendants with lanterns had been busily adjusting the harness of the horses while the landlord talked to Bathurst's secretary in the doorway of the inn. And yet, in the very midst of all this activity – and surrounded by people – Bathurst had simply disappeared.

There was a delay before a search was mounted because it occurred to no one that a man could just vanish under such circumstances. After searching the inn and the immediate surroundings the secretary approached Captain Klitzing, who authorized a thorough search for the missing man the following day. Rivers were dragged, the countryside was combed and buildings were scoured, but all in vain.

It was not until 16 December that a clue was forthcoming. Two peasant women found a pair of trousers in a local wood. The trousers were soaked with water and contained two bullet holes. One of the pockets revealed a note, in Bathurst's handwriting, to the effect that he feared danger from the Count d'Entraigues, a French double-agent. Despite offers of generous rewards no further clues came to light. Of course, the usual rumours circulated: he had been lost at sea, he had been murdered by his secretary, and so on. D'Entraigues apparently claimed that French agents had kidnapped Bathurst and taken him to the French garrison at Magdeburg, where he was murdered. Certainly, for propaganda purposes, this was the view that the British government wished to foster. To compound the mystery, an article appeared in January 1810 in a Hamburg newspaper announcing that Bathurst was alive and well, his friends having received a letter from him. The French newspaper *Moniteur* maintained that he had committed suicide, the British diplomatic service, it claimed, being composed of half-crazy fools. Bathurst had clearly taken on the guise of a political football, both British and French being anxious to use the circumstance of his disappearance to good account against each other.

It is often overlooked in assessments of Bathurst's case that he was a very natty dresser. During the course of his last earthly journey he wore a sable greatcoat lined in violet velvet with a fur cap to match. He also sported a valuable diamond scarf pin. At the time of his disappearance he had not been wearing the fur coat, yet Captain Klitzing could not find it among his belongings. Eventually it turned up, hidden in the cellar of a house belonging to a family called Schmidt. Frau Schmidt claimed it had been left at the post-house, where she had found it. Subsequently she gave it to her son Augustus, an habitual criminal. This lead is worth following up because someone claimed that Bathurst had actually been seen going off down the street where the Schmidts lived. Unfortunately, internal bureaucratic bickering over the handling of the investigations led to this promising avenue being neglected. Had Bathurst simply been the victim of opportunist street crime? The Schmidts were merely charged with theft of the coat.

In April 1810 Bathurst's mother arrived on the scene. Her presence served only to encourage certain dubious individuals with nothing to offer save itchy palms for the reward money. One interesting approach, however, was made by a woman called Hacker, who claimed to have met a man from Perleberg who told her that he had been paid a considerable sum of money to keep his mouth shut over something he knew concerning, as he put it, the Englishman's murder. Hacker and her husband had been close associates of Augustus Schmidt. But once again, this tantalizing connection was ignored.

What Mrs Bathurst did get was the personal assurance of Napoleon Bonaparte that he knew nothing of the matter. It is probable that he was speaking the truth, having far weightier matters than the elimination of a junior diplomat on his mind. Even if the French were responsible, the deed could well have been engineered by the French Secret Service without Napoleon's knowledge.

And so the matter rested – until 1952 when a skeleton was discovered during the demolition of a house in Perleberg. Investigation showed that the house had, at the time of Bathurst's disappearance, belonged to a man called Mertens who was employed at the White Swan Inn, where Bathurst had stayed. Naturally the skeleton could not be identified as Bathurst's and, as far as anyone could remember, Mertens had been of good character, although he was known to have been far wealthier than the nature of his employment at the White Swan should have allowed. Had Mertens, perhaps with the aid of Schmidt and the Hackers, robbed and murdered the Englishman? The skeleton's condition was suggestive of a violent death.

There is no proof that the skeleton was that of Bathurst. And, in a small early nineteenth-century community, it is likely that the lives of the inhabitants were closely intertwined. We cannot make too much of the probability that many of the minor characters in the drama enacted at Perleberg knew one another.

The case must remain a mystery. Bathurst's mother never gave up hope of his return, living out the remainder of her days in an agony of doubt as to whether her son was alive or dead. As a contemporary German commentator remarked, it was as if the ground had opened and swallowed Bathurst up, closing itself upon him without leaving the least trace behind.

'Buster' Crabb

It is only within recent years that British people have spoken of British 'spies'. Other countries, notably the Soviet Union or wartime opponents, are charged with spying. The British, for their part, admit to doing things through 'diplomatic channels'. Sometimes an admission is made to conducting 'intelligence' activities – but rarely to indulging in the nefarious activity of spying. The arrest in the Soviet Union of the British spy Greville Wynn, caught on the job in 1962, was reported with great indignation by the British press, in which Wynn was invariably referred to as a 'British businessman'. But when a spy is caught the circumstances can be whitewashed for a limited period only – depending, of course, on whether his captors decide to make his fate public knowledge. Nearly 35 years ago there occurred the disappearance of an ex-naval intelligence officer in decidedly fishy circumstances. To this day the fate of Lionel 'Buster' Crabb remains a mystery.

'Buster' Crabb was born in 1910. During the 1930s he had several jobs, including a spell as a merchant marine apprentice. The advent of the Second World War was a traumatic experience for most of his fellow countrymen, but Crabb was one of those few for whom the cataclysm provided opportunity and direction of purpose. Working his way through the Royal Naval Patrol Service, he acquired a commission and was sent to Gibraltar in 1942 as a bomb disposal officer. Working in Alexandria and Gibraltar it was his job, as a frogman, to work underwater at removing limpet mines which had been attached to the hulls of Royal Navy merchantmen by Italian divers. It was an unenviable task, but one at which Crabb excelled. His work in this sphere won him a George Cross and promotion to lieutenant-commander. It was during these activities that he suffered an injury to his left leg, an injury which left him with a distinctive scar.

The coming of peace in 1945 deprived him of his livelihood. Today, a man of his ability and experience would have been invaluable to any number of marine commercial enterprises, but in the years of austerity following the war there was no place for him. In 1950 he was involved in attempts to rescue the crew of the submarine *Truculent*, accidentally sunk in the Thames

Estuary. In 1956 he was to be found diving in Tobermory Bay in an attempt to trace a sunken Spanish galleon there. But diving assignments were few and far between. In any event he was now 46 and beginning to feel the strain. He took employment as a representative of a firm which supplied equipment to coffee bars.

Benjamin Bathurst, it will be remembered, was a flashy dresser and so was Crabb. His wardrobe was augmented with a monocle and a swordstick, the head of which was fashioned in the form of a gold crab. One of the golden rules for those engaged in covert activities is not to dress or behave in a manner likely to attract attention. Bathurst, Crabb and, as we shall see, Sidney Reilly all ignored this commandment.

It is likely that Crabb attracted a good deal of attention when he arrived, ostensibly on private business, in Portsmouth on 17 April 1956. He was accompanied by a man called Smith whose identity has never been satisfactorily established. The next day the Soviet leaders Nikolai Bulganin and Nikita Khrushchev arrived in Portsmouth aboard the revolutionary 12,000-ton warship *Ordzhonikidze* on a goodwill mission.

Crabb was out all day on the 18th. He also went out after breakfast on the 19th but failed to return in the evening. During the course of the 19th, the mysterious Mr Smith left the Sallyport Hotel, taking with him Crabb's luggage as well as his own. Special Branch later paid a visit to the hotel and, with surprising indiscretion, ripped out the pages in the register relevant to Crabb's period of stay and told the hotel staff to keep their mouths shut if they knew what was good for them. Having thus set the whole of Portsmouth talking, the authorities had some explaining to do. Significantly it was not until 29 April, a day after the departure of the Soviet visitors, that the Admiralty issued a statement, which said: 'He [Crabb] is presumed dead as a result of trials with certain underwater apparatus.' Here was the link necessary to complete the chain: 'Buster' Crabb – *Ordzhonikidze* – underwater 'trials'. The press made the most of what was called 'The Missing Frogman Mystery'.

It is well known that intelligence officers never retire. They may be no longer engaged on active duties, but from time to time they may be called upon to undertake investigative work – as Crabb himself had done in the past. Such work may not necessarily be of critical importance but it helps the authorities to keep in touch with its former operatives and to ensure their continued loyalty. It was believed that Crabb had been commissioned to check out the *Ordzhonikidze* and that the Russians had caught him.

He would have been the ideal man for the job. Apart from his unrivalled experience in underwater investigation, he was a civilian and could not be directly linked with the government if anything went wrong. And so Prime Minister Sir Anthony Eden, when pressed, declared: 'It would not be in the public interest to disclose the circumstances in which Commander Crabb is presumed to have met his death.' The statement also said that 'what was done was without the knowledge . . . of Her Majesty's Ministers.'

This served only to fan the flames of curiosity even more, and the aimless theorizing continued: he had been killed by Soviet frogmen; he had run into difficulties with his breathing apparatus; he had been captured by the crew of the *Ordzhonikidze* and taken back to the Soviet Union where he had been horribly tortured.

What the situation really demanded was a corpse, and one was conveniently forthcoming when, in June 1957, fishermen found a body in Chichester harbour. It was headless and without hands but there, on the remarkably well preserved left leg, was Crabb's distinctive wartime scar. The coroner expressed his satisfaction that the remains were those of Commander Crabb.

The fishermen's grisly catch followed hard on the heels of the passage of a number of Soviet submarines through the English Channel en route to the Near East. It is not altogether impossible that the Russians jettisoned the body, and a theory was developed which held that Crabb had indeed been captured and taken to the Soviet Union where he was given the opportunity to work with the Soviet Navy, doing what he loved and knew best. To put the bloodhounds off the scent, a suitably doctored body had been prepared as human jetsam.

It is undoubtedly suspicious that the parts of the body which would have rendered positive identification a certainty – the hands and the head – were missing. It is as likely that the British dumped the body where it was found, purely to discourage continued speculation. In fact, the one clear thread running through the entire case is the embarrassment of the British government.

The truth is that Crabb had been spotted by the Russians in the vicinity of the warship – a sighting which caused a minor diplomatic incident. The Russians, in the interests of their goodwill initiative, did not make too much of it, but the exercise was a silly one for the British government to indulge in, considering the circumstances. The Russians would hardly have drawn attention to Crabb and then proceeded to kidnap or harm him. The British, however, would have every reason for silencing him. He had bungled his job and placed his erstwhile employers in a difficult position. As soon as he returned to shore the hungry newspapermen would be swarming around him. Realizing that he had been seen, and anticipating the Soviet reaction, the authorities may well have decided that Crabb was a man who had outlived his usefulness, and disposed of him accordingly. Such a theory would certainly fit the available facts. It would also go some way towards explaining why the government dossier on the affair was not released within the terms of the 30-year rule. Whatever the true facts of the case, the issue, after the passage of 30 years, is still considered too sensitive a subject for open discussion.

above: Colonel Fawcett's companions at Dead Horse Camp, from where he wrote his last letter.
below: Mallory and Irvine (back row, left and second from left) pictured with the other members of the Everest expedition in which they lost their lives.

Buster Crabb, the frogman who disappeared in mysterious circumstances during the visit of the Soviet leaders Bulganin and Khrushchev to Britain in 1956.

above: The Arrival of the Englishmen in Virginia. A contemporary engraving after a drawing by John White, showing Roanoke Island. One hundred and twenty colonists vanished from this settlement between 1586 and 1590.

below: Allied troops at Gallipoli, scene of the mysterious disappearance of 267 men of the I/5th Norfolk Regiment during an assault on enemy lines.

Lord and Lady Lucan (*above*) are at the centre of one of the most intriguing mysteries of this century. Lord Lucan went missing on 7 November 1974, the night on which his children's nanny, Sandra Rivett (*right*), was found murdered in the basement of his estranged wife's home.

Sidney Reilly

During the course of their visit to Britain, Bulganin and Khrushchev were asked to clear up another mystery – one of 30 years' standing which involved a man of whose activities as a spy there was no doubt, the man who has been dubbed 'Ace of Spies': Sidney Reilly.

A television series, portraying his life, made much of his reputation as a gambler, womanizer and all-round exhibitionist. In so doing it missed many of the finer points of his character. Such was his significance that, despite the lapse of 60 years, the Russians' early efforts at *glasnost* did not stretch as far as providing an explanation for Reilly's disappearance in the Soviet Union in 1927.

Sidney Reilly was born a Jew, Georgi Rosenblum, near Odessa in the Ukraine in 1874. He later changed his name to Reilly, arguing that it would assist him in his profession of spy because few people would trust anyone with a Jewish name, while the name of Reilly was sufficiently Irish to suggest that he was anti-British.

He took his first assignment on behalf of the British government in 1897. It was to ascertain whether the Russians had any objections to Britain drilling for oil in Persia. Ultimately his 'diplomatic' work in this respect was to lead to the foundation of the British Petroleum empire. It is important to understand that Reilly was never a member of the British Secret Intelligence Service. He began, and ended, his career as a freelance, although he made no secret of the fact that he would have loved to be taken onto the staff, as it were, as an official agent. The freelance arrangement suited the British admirably. They had working for them perhaps the finest spy of all time, yet their obligation to him and to his welfare was nil. As well as the finest spy of all time, Reilly was the most shabbily treated by his employers.

During his early years he plied his trade in the guise of a pedlar of patent medicines. As time went on he ploughed more and more of his own money into the support of his spying activities and, ultimately, beggared himself. He was a deeply sensitive man, cut to the quick when affection proferred was not returned, or when a confidence trustingly shared was betrayed. In some ways he was as much the tool of women as their seducer.

Margaret, his first wife, remained a thorn in his side long after they had drifted apart. On one celebrated occasion in 1912 he offered her the then enormous sum of £10,000 to leave him alone.

Much valuable espionage work was performed by Reilly in the years immediately prior to the First World War. As only he could, he managed to obtain an interest in the German ship-building concern Blohm and Voss. In this capacity he was able to peruse all developments, designs and modifications to the German fleet in its pre-war naval build-up. He dutifully passed on all this information to his masters in London. But it was the outbreak of the First World War itself which allowed Reilly the leeway to indulge himself in the colourful exploits that were to create a legend.

It is difficult during this period of Reilly's activities to distinguish between fact and fiction, but at the most conservative estimate his achievements were startling. On many occasions he was dropped behind the German lines, not only masquerading as a German soldier but, at one time, even enlisting in the ranks. He also met Kaiser Wilhelm and sat in on German High Command briefings. Perhaps his most important coup during the war was his acquisition of the plans for the massive U-boat onslaught on British shipping in 1917 – intelligence which proved crucial to the final outcome. Had Reilly's career ended in 1918 there would have been enough to ensure his immortality, but there was destined to be another chapter – the final one – which would help to explain the enigma that was Sidney Reilly.

Reilly's first love was Russia. During the course of his Persian assignment in 1897 his primary concern had been to safeguard Russian interests. It was because of his interest in Russia that he came, eventually, to be distrusted in Whitehall. And because of his uncanny knack of working so well with those upon whom he was spying, there were fears that he might, from time to time, be practising as a double-agent. Espionage is, indeed, an involved and complicated profession.

In 1917, at a critical stage in the First World War, there occurred one of the momentous events of modern times – the Russian Revolution. Apart from the profound political and economic consequences for Europe, Lenin and the Bolsheviks had made it clear that they wanted no further part in the war. In the first of his two personal Russian campaigns, Reilly was sent to Moscow by Lloyd George to try to persuade the Russians to maintain a second front or, in the event of a refusal, to overthrow the Bolsheviks by subversive means.

In an effort to ascertain the state of play on the subject of participation in the war, Reilly, upon his arrival in Moscow, went to the Kremlin, knocked on the front door, and asked if Lenin was in. He wasn't and Reilly promptly went underground with a view to organizing anti-Bolshevik elements. Displaying what was even for him immense energy and organizational ability, he created single-handed a sound, practical model for the overthrow of Bolshevism which he came to abhor as he witnessed more and more its appalling consequences on his beloved homeland. But all his work came to nothing through a blunder by the French Secret Service. Cognisant of Reilly's schemes, it accidentally told all to a French journalist who was also, it transpired, a member of the Communist Party.

Reilly had no option but to make a hasty departure from Russia, returning home to face a crisis in his financial affairs. In an effort to stave off complete ruin he went to the United States in 1923, but was unsuccessful in obtaining money owed to him through various business deals. His plight had arisen through neglect of his business affairs while undertaking his unpaid work on behalf of the British government. He was now at the crossroads as far as his future was concerned. He was 50 years of age, he had barely a penny to his name, and he had been told by the Secret Intelligence Service that they had no use for him as an official, permanent member of their staff. All he had left was his love for Russia, the land of his birth. And so it was that he took the momentous decision to return there.

Lenin had died and the Bolsheviks were split in their support for Trotsky and Stalin. Reilly saw this schism as an opportunity to step in and break the Bolsheviks' stranglehold. The British government was, despite its rejection of him, only too anxious to provide him with encouragement in this adventure. He was taking a grave risk, for his identity had been disclosed following the debacle of 1918, and he had, in his absence, been sentenced to death.

His success – and his safety – depended upon 'The Trust', a strong, secret organization of anti-Bolsheviks which included many influential people who were above suspicion. To make any progress in its aims it needed a leader, and Reilly sought to fill that need. Accordingly, ignoring the risks, he left for the Soviet Union in the autumn of 1925. On 27 September of that year he sent a postcard, indicating that he was in Moscow. That postcard was his last communication. Nothing more was heard from him. He had vanished.

Likely explanations about his fate are numerous. For Sidney Reilly nothing was beyond the bounds of possibility. That he had been betrayed seems certain, for 'The Trust' was really a tool of the Bolsheviks, employed to sniff out opposition. But had he been caught and, if so, what had happened to him? The official story released in the Soviet press was that he had been shot while attempting to cross the Finnish border and that his identity had not come to light until later. It seems strange, if this were the case, that the Russians made no attempt to maximize the propaganda potential of the incident.

Naturally the British government disowned him, so it was left for the rumours to circulate. He had been captured by the GPU (forerunner of the KGB), interrogated and shot. He was in prison, in Orlovsky, and insane. He was in China, working as a Soviet agent. Sightings continued up to the end of the Second World War (when he would have been over 70 years of age) in the Soviet Union, the United States and the Middle East.

His fate will never be known for sure. But it is certainly not improbable that he arranged his own disappearance. Men with similar problems to himself have done so. It is even possible that he could have defected to the Russians. Most commentators consider this unthinkable, but we must bear in mind Reilly's over-riding concern for the welfare of his homeland. Did he see a role for himself, working from within the Bolshevik system, as a moderating influence? This is the option which people will find the most appealing. It fits the man and the myths surrounding him admirably. Whether or not it represents the truth becomes almost immaterial.

3

CROWDS AWAY

The Lost Colony

Sir Walter Raleigh is a man with many claims to fame. Among his listed achievements are the introduction to Europe of both tobacco and the potato. Crowning all, of course, in the popular imagination is the occasion upon which he spread his cloak in the gutter for the benefit of Queen Elizabeth. The fact that there is no truth in any of it has not detracted from his reputation. Raleigh did demonstrate great skill in writing verse and has taken his place, quite rightly, alongside Donne and Marvell as one of the great metaphysical poets of his day. His other great interest in life – overseas exploration – proved to be less of a success and led ultimately to his execution.

Yet even in this sphere of activity he has managed to acquire and retain more than his fair share of the credit. He preferred not to accompany the voyages of discovery which he organized, and viewed such ventures largely as a means of self-aggrandizement. Much of the early pioneer work of exploration of North American coastal waters was done by Raleigh's step-brother, Humphrey Gilbert, who nurtured a genuine desire to see English settlers in the New World. With the Spanish preoccupied in exploiting the wealth of South America, the English had a free hand in tentative exploration further north. In 1583 Gilbert took possession of Newfoundland in Queen Elizabeth's name, although no attempt at a permanent settlement was made. On the homeward voyage Gilbert's ship was lost in a storm and it fell to Raleigh to continue his work. The difference was that while Gilbert had been primarily concerned with establishing settlements, Raleigh's major incentive, like that of the Spanish, lay in the discovery of gold.

Vanished!

With the Spanish dominating the American coastline as far north as Florida, Raleigh had to concentrate his activities further up the seaboard, but well to the south of Newfoundland, which was infested by fog and hostile Indians. In March 1584 he successfully procured from Queen Elizabeth a patent granting him permission to explore 'such remote, heathen and barbarous lands, countries and territories not actually possessed of any Christian prince, nor inhabited by Christian people.' One fifth of all the treasure he found was to go to the crown.

The expedition (unaccompanied by Raleigh himself) comprised two ships captained by Philip Amadas and Arthur Barlowe. They left England in April 1584 and, negotiating the Atlantic via the Canary Islands, put in to a haven about 125 miles up the coastline from Florida. Subsequent exploration showed that the land, which was fertile and abundant with game, was not the mainland after all but a long island, Roanoke Island. They christened it Virginia.

During their sojourn they encountered a tribe of friendly Indians and cultivated the friendship of the chief, Granganimeo. Bearing glowing reports of this new land and of the welcome they had received, the members of the expedition arrived back in England in September. As a result of this encouraging news, a fleet of seven ships under Sir Richard Grenville set sail the following spring. A hundred men under the command of Ralph Lane were put ashore in Virginia with the object of establishing a colony there during the next 12 months.

Lane and his companions discovered that not all the Indians were friendly, the various tribes being constantly at war with one another. The colonists were also dependent upon the goodwill of the Indians for the provision of food. Granganimeo was now dead, his son Pemisapan reigning in his stead. Pemisapan was not quite as friendly as his father and did his best to destroy the embryonic settlement. During one of the fights which ensued, Pemisapan was killed, but the English were still in very poor repair, being unable to fend for themselves without the Indians' help.

It was with great joy, therefore, that they greeted Sir Francis Drake and his fleet of 23 ships, Drake having taken time off from his piratical exploits in the West Indies in order to call on them. The condition of the men led Drake to agree to evacuate the

38

colony. This proved difficult, however, for a savage storm left the fleet severely damaged. Drake did manage to put his ships to sea, but at the cost of leaving 15 colonists on land.

Drake arrived in England with the remnants of the Virginian colonists in July 1586. Although the exercise had been a disaster, there was evidence that considerable deposits of copper were waiting to be exploited, with the added promise of rich pearl fishing among the inlets dotting the coastline.

Accordingly, Raleigh sent out John White with 150 men the following year. Upon his arrival White attempted to trace the 15 men who had been left behind the year before. The Indians, who seemed to have regained their friendly disposition, advised him that the Englishmen had been attacked by another hostile tribe which had killed some of their number, the survivors fleeing to a nearby island from which they had disappeared. On this somewhat discouraging note White sailed for England, leaving another colony of 120 men and women – and his own granddaughter, christened Virginia, the first white child to be born in North America.

White left for England in 1586 but was prevented from returning to Virginia the following year as planned. War with Spain was brewing and there followed a government embargo on ships setting sail from British ports. In the spring of 1588 White did contrive to encourage two captains to break the embargo and set sail on a re-provisioning expedition, but they were compelled to put back into port after coming off worst in an encounter with a French vessel.

Even after the destruction of the Armada very little was done to get a relief expedition under way. The truth was that Raleigh was becoming disillusioned with the Virginian design. He had new fish to fry nearer home, in Ireland, where it was possible to build up vast estates at much less risk. And so it was not until the spring of 1590 that White finally got under way again. Even then the three captains commissioned for the task were more interested in privateering, preying in particular upon Spanish shipping. Eventually, Virginia was reached in August of 1590.

Upon landing on Roanoke Island, White found the settlement to be deserted. The primitive houses he had left in 1586 had been replaced by a pallisade. He had agreed with the colonists that if they were compelled to leave the settlement they should carve

39

the name of their destination on the trunk of a tree, and that if they were in any danger a cross should be carved above it. On one of the corner posts of the pallisade was carved the word 'Croatoan', a friendly Indian village 50 miles to the north. With relief White noted that there was no cross carved above the name.

But his relief was short-lived. The season was, by now, too far advanced to permit much time to be spent in excursions along the coastline. A cursory search was made, but weather conditions took a turn for the worse so all three ships turned tail and made for a friendlier coast. White was unable to find anyone else – least of all Raleigh – to finance a further expedition and, incredible as it may seem, the Virginians were left to their fate.

And just what was their fate? The colonists had disappeared without trace. There was no indication that they had been in any danger – although they must have been on the verge of starvation. What must their feelings have been when first one, then two and three years passed with no sign of relief? Their only hope of survival lay with the Indians.

It is believed that the settlers divided into two groups, a small party remaining in Croatoan to await the return of White, while the main body moved further inland to the swamplands of present-day southern Virginia, where they lived for 20 years, intermingling with the Indians until they were almost wiped out by the warlike Powhatans. Certainly, many legends concerning white tribes with English names have been handed down to us.

That the disappearance of the colonists is mysterious cannot be denied, although it can be explained by other than super-natural reasons. The true horror of the story lies in the fact that civilized Europeans could be callously abandoned in the way that they were. It must be remembered, nonetheless, that the sixteenth century was an age in which death was a daily occur-rence. Many critics pointed out that the settlers had been aware of the risks involved and had only themselves to blame. Others blamed the sea captains. The sea captains blamed the merchants. The merchants blamed Raleigh. And Raleigh, rather unwisely, blamed the Queen.

Like a present-day politician, Raleigh parried any awkward questions with the bland statement that Virginia remained an outpost which could, at any future time, be contacted with a view to development. Some people such as Francis Bacon were unimpressed, Bacon himself referring to the 'guiltless blood of many miserable persons'. But the American continent was to exact a terrible revenge. Raleigh was assigned to the Tower of London on charges of treachery by the new king, James I, but in 1616 he was released on the understanding that he would lead an expedition to discover El Dorado. His son, who accompanied him, was killed on the Orinoco in a skirmish with Spaniards and Raleigh returned home empty handed. His last expedition, in October 1618, was a short one, to the scaffold.

The Norfolks

A disappearance of people *en masse* of a far more sinister nature occurred in 1915 at Gallipoli, when over 200 men of the I/5th Norfolk regiment vanished from sight.

Gallipoli, a peninsula jutting out into the Aegean Sea, is part of Turkey. The Gallipoli campaign of the First World War was undertaken by the Allies to relieve the pressure on the Russian Army in the Caucasus. It lasted for only 12 months, from February 1915 until January 1916. Poorly led and equipped, it proved a fiasco, rivalling in ineptitude and disorganization the most disastrous initiatives of the Western Front.

The main battlefield of the campaign was the Suvla Plain, set against a backcloth of desolate hills. The Allies lay exposed on the plain while the Turks were embedded in the hills. The commander-in-chief, Sir Ian Hamilton, held to a strategy throughout the campaign of mass assaults on the Turks' entrenched positions. When not engaged in these misguided forays the allied troops were incarcerated in trenches, in conditions even worse than those prevailing on the Western Front.

By way of preparation for one of the all-out assaults, scheduled for the evening of 12 August 1915, the British 163rd Brigade of Territorials was ordered forward to mop up any snipers in forward Turkish positions. The 163rd – comprising the I/8th Hampshires, I/5th Suffolks, and I/4th and I/5th Norfolks – moved out with inadequate artillery cover in the late afternoon. The main body of the 163rd came under heavy machinegun fire and went to ground. However, the I/5th Norfolks on the right of the line of advance were able to press on. What happened next was described by Sir Ian Hamilton in a report to Lord Kitchener:

> The fighting grew hotter, and the ground became more wooded and broken. At this stage many men were wounded or grew exhausted with thirst. These found their way back to camp during the night. But the Colonel [Beauchamp], with 16 officers and 250 men, still kept pushing forward, driving the enemy before him. Amongst these ardent souls was part of a fine company enlisted from the King's Sandringham estates. Nothing more was seen or heard of any of them. They charged into the forest and were lost to sight or sound. None of them ever came back.

Two hundred and sixty-seven men had vanished without trace.

Colour is added to the story by the strange tale told by a company of New Zealanders who had witnessed the occurrence. They spoke of seeing a dense, solid-looking cloud, shaped like a loaf of bread, settle on the ground in the path of the advancing Norfolks. The brigade entered the cloud which, as soon as the last soldier had been swallowed up, rose into the sky where, in company with a number of similar clouds, it drifted away. The incident is made even stranger by the fact that but for these half dozen or so strangely shaped clouds, the day was a clear one.

Half a century later three of the original witnesses to this event produced a signed statement confirming what they had seen. Sceptics have made much of one or two factual errors contained – inevitably, with the passing of 50 years – in the statement. For example, reference is made to the I/4th Norfolks, instead of the I/5ths, and the date of the event is given as 21 August, as opposed to 12 August.

Of more use to critics is the acknowledgement that the whole process involving men and cloud took place within about three-quarters of an hour, during which time most of the brigade was lost from view. In 45 minutes much can happen on a battlefield, and on this understanding it is quite possible that officers and men were cut to pieces. On the Western Front the loss of 267 infantrymen during the course of an assault would have been hardly worth mentioning. Yet the incident at Gallipoli was sufficiently curious for the British to press the Turks for their views on the matter at the conclusion of the war in 1918.

The Turks denied all knowledge of the I/5th Norfolks and were unable to produce any prisoners. Further enquiries did actually lead to the discovery of a number of bodies, crudely buried by the farmer on whose land they had been found – about 120 in total. Although they were positively identified as men belonging to the I/5ths, this figure still leaves more than 140 unaccounted for. If the I/5th Norfolks had been cut down by enemy fire during the time they were obscured from their comrades' view, it is likely that they would have fallen in a relatively confined – and well defined – area. And so we have another example of a supposedly rational solution merely compounding a mystery.

The Ninth Legion

The stories of the missing Norfolks and of Raleigh's lost colony are the best known of what we might term disappearances *en masse*. But, as ever, there are others which have not achieved quite such a degree of notoriety, although the circumstances surrounding them are no less inexplicable. Running a close third is the strange tale of the Ninth Legion.

The Romans never fully succeeded in subjugating the ancient Britons, and in AD 61 the occupying Roman army was badly pressed. Under Boadicea the hitherto disorganized opposition to the invasion took on the semblance of a unified front. Against the horde of barbarians assembled by the Iceni queen there stood only four Roman legions: the Second at Gloucester, the Ninth at Lincoln, and the Fourteenth and Twentieth which, at the time of the uprising, were in the west under the command of the governor of the province, Suetonius, who was attempting to subdue the Celts.

Colchester bore the brunt of the initial onslaught and was burned to the ground with its Roman inhabitants and its hated British collaborators. The Ninth Legion marched out from Lincoln in an attempt to stem the revolt. Boadicea decided to meet it head-on. The Ninth was overwhelmed by sheer weight of numbers and cut to pieces. The commander, Petrilius Ceralius, was happy to escape with only his cavalry intact.

Boadicea went on to sack both London and St Albans but was eventually routed by Suetonius, who had made a forced march from Wales. With a disciplined force of 10,000 men he overcame Boadicea's army of an estimated 80,000, destroying it to a man. Boadicea took poison as a preferable alternative to capture.

One uprising had been quelled, but others took its place. The Iceni had traditionally been thought of as one of the more placid British tribes. One of the most warlike was the Brigantes, who continually rose against their Roman masters. By the time of Hadrian's succession in AD 117 the Brigantes, aided by their allies the Novantae from the far north, had become uncontrollable. In the year AD 121 Hadrian visited Britain personally and instituted the massive construction project which bears his name: the building of a wall 73 miles long between the Tyne and the Solway.

The thinking behind this revolved not so much around the need to keep out the tribes from southern Scotland as the desirability of driving a wedge between them and their Brigante allies. That this work was thought necessary may have some bearing on the sudden disappearance of the Ninth Legion.

The continuous warfare waged by the Brigantes is very poorly documented, having taken place in the wilds of northern Britain, so distant from the populous and prosperous south-east. To the Ninth Legion, reconstituted and removed to York, fell the unenviable task of maintaining law and order. In their efforts to do so it seems that a terrible fate befell them for, at about the time of Hadrian's accession, they disappeared from recorded history. In what was probably the year AD 122 the York fortress was taken over by the Sixth Legion, sent over from Germany for this specific task. The disappearance of their predecessors is one of the greatest mysteries of all time and has remained unsolved to this day.

The most likely explanation is that the jinxed Ninth was routed by the Brigantes in much the same way that Boadicea had defeated them 50 years before – only this time the British finished the job. Perhaps a relatively small number of Romans, retained in the garrison at York, escaped the slaughter which would have involved the ultimate in ignominy: the loss of the Eagle – the Legion's military standard and emblem.

To Rome, with a civilization steeped in superstition, the Ninth was clearly bad medicine. No second attempt at reconstruction was made and the Ninth was allowed to rest in peace. This crushing defeat was hushed-up in order to avoid a general panic. The Ninth was simply erased from the record books.

4

LORD LUCAN IS MISSING

The name of Lord Lucan used always to be associated with the Crimean War. Together with fellow noblemen Cardigan and Raglan, Lucan was part and parcel of all that was great about the British Empire, the spirit of which was immortalized by Tennyson in 'The Charge of the Light Brigade'. In this celebrated example of British military incompetence, Lucan played only a supporting role, covering the light brigade's retreat. The famous charge was actually led by Lord Cardigan who, as a result of a slight misunderstanding with his commanding officer, Lord Raglan, had attacked the wrong, heavily defended position. Yet the myth of glory and worthwhile self-sacrifice persisted down through the years until the late 1950s when, with Britain finally relinquishing her grand imperial role, the matter was all but forgotten. No longer did schoolboys pore over atlases which depicted a third of the world's land mass (and, of course, all the water) as coming under British control. And a further 20 years were to pass before the name of Lucan was, once again, to be held up to public gaze.

The seventh Earl of Lucan, Richard John Bingham, had, like the third earl, enjoyed a military career, although only in the capacity of a national serviceman (albeit in the prestigious Coldstream Guards). During his time in the army Lucan developed an activity that was to lead to his downfall. Largely as a result of the boredom which grew from the inactivity of national service life, he became a compulsive gambler. Had he been posted to any of the growing number of colonial trouble spots, such as Kenya or Malaya, other matters would have occupied his mind.

Upon leaving the army he went into the City, a natural consequence of his interest in gambling. Following a 'lucky streak' at the card tables, however, he turned his back on a successful career with a leading merchant bank and set up as a professional gambler. This was a doubly risky decision to take because Lucan was not known for frugal living. Regular jaunts to Monte Carlo and St Moritz contributed to an expansive and expensive lifestyle.

At 28 he married Veronica Duncan, a girl who, if not quite up to the level of Lucan's own social standing, was well-bred and the pair seemed well-matched. Yet over the ensuing 10 years their relationship deteriorated to the point of no return. Although Veronica bore children she also had a nanny to look after them. Her husband had many interests which she did not share (including the extravagance of power-boat racing, for which he had his own boat specially constructed), and there were the endless evenings spent alone while he was 'working' at the gaming tables.

Whatever the reason, Veronica's mental health declined to such an extent that her family and friends encouraged her to seek psychiatric advice. Domestic tensions led, finally, to the Lucans separating in 1973. By this time there were three children – two girls and a boy – and a bitter wrangle over custody ensued. Judgement had to be made in favour of either a mother who was in constant need of psychiatric attention or a father who was a professional gambler. Veronica won, with Lucan being allowed limited access.

By the autumn of 1974 it seemed to Lucan's friends that he was going to pieces. His efforts to win custody of the children continued, occupying his time to the exclusion of all else. Had he still been working in the City the strains and stresses of a normal working day would have taken their toll of time and energy. Instead, Lucan's waking hours were spent on the issue which was rapidly becoming an obsession. His luck at the gaming tables also deserted him and he ran heavily into debt. In October 1974 his estranged wife acquired the latest in a long line of children's nannies, a young woman – also separated from her husband – called Sandra Rivett.

The whole truth of what happened on the night of 7 November 1974 will probably never be known. What is certain is that on the

47

evening in question, towards 10pm, Lady Lucan, screaming hysterically and covered with blood, ran into the Plumber's Arms pub in Lower Belgrave Street, London. The staff and customers, after calling both for the police and an ambulance, managed to ascertain that in addition to the apparent attack on Lady Lucan herself, the new nanny had been murdered.

The police had to make a forced entry to Lady Lucan's home at Number 46. There was blood everywhere – except in the children's rooms, where they slept on, unharmed. The most gruesome sight was that of the family cat, happily lapping up blood from the basement floor. The lifeless, blood-soaked body of Sandra Rivett was found stuffed in a sack. She had been beaten to death with a length of lead piping. The search for Lord Lucan was on.

At 11.30 that evening Lucan was, in fact, calling on close family friends, the Maxwell-Scotts, in Uckfield, Sussex. At home alone, Susan Maxwell-Scott listened in shocked disbelief as Lucan told her his version of events at Lower Belgrave Street. He had, he said, been walking past Number 46 when, glancing through the window, he had caught sight of Veronica struggling with a man. By the time he got into the house the man was no longer there. He found only Veronica, screaming hysterically, and Sandra Rivett's body. While he rushed upstairs to check on the children, Veronica ran out of the house screaming 'Help me . . . he's murdered the nanny!' At this Lucan panicked, realizing the invidious position he was in. He fled to Uckfield, pausing only to telephone his mother, asking her to look after the children.

During the two hours he spent with Mrs Maxwell-Scott, Lucan wrote two letters to another friend, Bill Shand-Kydd, in which he explained what had happened, adding that he intended to 'lie doggo for a bit'. Despite Mrs Maxwell-Scott's entreaties to stay, he left her at around 1.15am, driving off in a dark-coloured saloon car – an old Ford Corsair which was later found abandoned in Newhaven. The car had been borrowed from a friend, Michael Stoop, two weeks prior to the murder for a purpose Lucan refused to disclose. He did go so far as to write to Stoop to apologize for not returning it. Although he kept the letter, Stoop destroyed the envelope with its tell-tale postmark.

Incredibly both Susan Maxwell-Scott and her husband Ian failed to contact the police for a full day after Lucan's late-night visit. When they did call someone it was Shand-Kydd, to ask him if he had received the letters Lucan had written to him and which their seven-year-old daughter had posted. Shand-Kydd took the letters to the police – one of the few instances, the police felt, in which their investigations were positively assisted by the actions of Lucan's circle of friends.

Meanwhile the police were concentrating their search for Lucan in the Newhaven area. Although they were not discounting the theory that he may have committed suicide, and were combing beaches beneath sheer cliffs and scrubland on the Sussex Downs, detectives remained aware of the fact that the Ford Corsair had been abandoned near the yacht marina and the Newhaven-Dieppe ferry terminal. Extensive enquiries were therefore made on the Continent.

What it all amounted to was that a murder had been committed and Lucan, by reason of his flight, was presumed guilty by police, press and public. The inquest into Sandra Rivett's death, a full seven months after the event, seemed more like a trial for murder with Lucan as the absentee defendant. At the inquest Lady Lucan gave her version of events.

At around nine o'clock in the evening it was her custom to make herself a cup of tea. On the evening of Thursday 7 November, however, Sandra Rivett had offered to make it. After about a quarter of an hour Veronica had left her bedroom, where she was watching television, to go down to the kitchen to see why Sandra was taking so long. As she reached the ground floor someone rushed at her, raining down blows on her head. She screamed, and a voice she identified as that of her estranged husband told her to shut up. But she fought back as her attacker thrust a gloved hand into her mouth and tried to strangle her. Then, as suddenly as it had started, the fight stopped. Lucan helped his wife upstairs. While he was in the bathroom Veronica took the opportunity to run out of the house and down to the pub.

It was certainly a curious story. Things looked black for Lucan. The ill-feeling which existed between Veronica and himself over custody of the children was motive enough. He could have learned of her routine of making her way down the dark staircase each night at nine o'clock to make tea and lain in wait. Something he did not know was that Sandra Rivett, whose night off was Thursday and who would not normally have been in the house on Thursday evening, had that very week exchanged Thursday for Wednesday. The murderer, hearing someone descend the staircase at nine o'clock on that Thursday night, must have been certain that that person was Veronica, Lady Lucan. Only when it was too late did he realize his error.

Lady Lucan had named her husband as her attacker, and the presumption was made that he was also the murderer of Sandra Rivett, despite one or two serious flaws in Veronica's story. Would her husband really have helped her upstairs and attended to her after attacking her so ferociously? And there was no mention in her statement of her discovery of Sandra Rivett's body, although she volunteered the information on her arrival at the Plumber's Arms that the nanny was dead. Indeed, for a time Lady Lucan herself was on the list of suspects as the killer.

There was also an element of doubt attached to the matter of the Ford Corsair. Had, as the police suspected, Lucan borrowed it to use as a getaway car, in the boot of which he had intended to secrete his wife's body? He had taken to watching the house in Lower Belgrave Street, ostensibly to ensure that the children were all right. The unremarkable Ford Corsair, his friends argued, could have been intended for this purpose instead of his own distinctive Mercedes. But his visits to Lower Belgrave Street would also have enabled him to compile an accurate dossier on the routine activities of the occupants.

As expected, and to the horror of Lucan's friends, the inquest jury found that Sandra Rivett had been murdered by Lord Lucan. Veronica's family and friends felt that justice had been done. The sole remaining problem was to find him. But was he alive or dead? There are two opposing schools of thought. As a 'man of honour', an English nobleman, he may have done the honourable thing and taken his own life. This is an unlikely possibility by virtue of the fact that he didn't have to travel to Newhaven, a European communications terminal, to do it. It seems much more likely that he took his chances on living. A professional gambler, he had grown accustomed to taking risks; and this, the biggest gamble of all, must surely have appealed to him.

Until the coroner's verdict was announced he probably did as he said he would do, 'lie doggo'. The bleak outcome left him no choice but to arrange for his own disappearance and to take up a new life under another name – perhaps even with a new face. To do so he needed help which, according to the police, he would have found no difficulty in obtaining. A particularly unfortunate feature of the murder investigation was the lack of sympathy between the police and the upper stratum of society in which the Lucans moved. More than one officer likened the aristocracy to the Mafia with its code of silence. There were several instances in which it was felt that interested parties were insufficiently appreciative of the gravity of the affair, although it is another matter to accuse them of complicity in shielding Lucan from justice.

Sightings of Lucan continue to be reported all over the world. He has been 'seen' in both North and South America, Australia, South Africa, Ireland (where he owns a substantial estate) and the Seychelles. From time to time bodies washed ashore on the Sussex coastline bring his name back to the headlines and hearken back to the suicide theory. A 1989 British tabloid newspaper campaign to find him spawned claims that he is masquerading as a car salesman in west London and a taxi driver in Chester. He has also been spotted in the unlikely surroundings of a McDonalds hamburger restaurant in Kensington, London. Even after 15 years Lucan's disappearance is still hot news.

Alternative theories of the murder abound. Publicity seekers have brought forward claims that a second man, as Lucan had said, was in the house. It has also been claimed that Lucan himself did not perform the murder but hired someone to do it. Only two people know what actually happened on that November evening in 1974: Lord and Lady Lucan. Until such time as Lord Lucan reappears, it is the testimony of his wife which will be generally accepted as representing the truth.

Veronica herself believes her husband to be alive. She says she talked to Lucan after he had attacked her and that he admitted to having killed Sandra Rivett. He had only stopped his attack on her because he was emotionally and physically exhausted. More of Lucan's friends are now willing to take the view that his instincts as a gambler and fighter would argue against his having taken his own life.

A personal view would be that the abandonment of the Ford Corsair at Newhaven was nothing more than a blind. Lucan

51

wanted the police to believe that he had indeed fled to France; and Newhaven, just 15 miles from his port of call at Uckfield, suited his purpose admirably. While the police were scouring the Continent for Lucan alive, and the offshore waters for Lucan dead, he was able to lie low, perhaps even in Newhaven itself. If he was the premeditated murderer the police thought him to be, then his plans would already have been laid: a short-term plan involving temporary shelter, and a long-term plan for his disappearance and the acquisition of a new identity. If his story were true, then he would at least have a breathing space in which to make preparations for the future.

It is probable that the world at large figured as little in Lucan's long-term plans as it did in the short-term. Lucan, the archetypal English aristocrat, in the Australian outback? On the streets of Brooklyn? With Ronald Biggs in Brazil? No: Lord Lucan is alive and well – and living in England. What safer place for an Englishman to hide? It is tempting to think that one day he will emerge into the open. It is tempting also to conclude with a comparison between the third and seventh Earls of Lucan, both of whom attained a degree of notoriety through their involvement in misdirected assaults.

5

ABSENT MEMBERS

Victor Grayson

It is one thing for a nondescript member of the public to disappear and quite another for a celebrity to vanish. It is only too true that the intensity of an official search for a missing person depends, quite often, upon the intensity of the interest shown by the media. The celebrity status of a missing person is very naturally an indicator of the length of time which the disappearancee can expect to command public attention. Victor Grayson's status as a former Member of Parliament has ensured that his disappearance has retained headline status from the 1920s to the present day.

Grayson's case is interesting, in the first instance, because it demonstrates how incorrect facts – with no basis in truth whatsoever – can become fixed in the public mind until, with the passage of time, they are accepted as the truth. The circumstances of Victor Grayson's disappearance, as agreed by several distinguished researchers, are that one August day in 1920 he boarded a train to travel from Liverpool to Hull. When the train pulled into Hull Paragon station, however, Grayson was not on it. He had disappeared without trace, and no rational explanation could be found. A curious case indeed.

The case also illustrates the problems raised by reported sightings of the missing person. For 25 years after his disappearance Grayson was being 'seen' all over the world – in tube trains, on buses, in Australia, and so on. But just how many of these sightings were genuine, and how many were cases of mistaken identity? Over the years, for example, I have seen some people who looked remarkably like myself. One such person almost looked more like myself than I did. The close resemblance left me speechless. Years later I saw him again, and the likeness was much less pronounced. The difference lay in the ageing process: he had lost no hair whereas my hairline was receding; I wore spectacles while he did not; he had developed a skin complaint which rendered his skin rather red and blotchy, while my complexion had remained much the same. Old friends who 'recognized' Victor Grayson many years after his disappearance were not seeing Grayson himself. They were simply identifying with the memory of Grayson, and were putting their own interpretation on the way in which he would have aged.

Born in Liverpool of working-class parents, Victor Grayson entered Parliament in 1907 via the Colne Valley by-election. The Liberal incumbent, Sir James Kitson, had retired to the House of Lords at the age of 71, leaving his seat available for a three-way contest between Liberal, Tory and Socialist. The votes were remarkably evenly distributed with Grayson scraping home by a margin of 153.

In the House of Commons the new MP proved to be an uncompromising Socialist who had little time for the embryonic Labour Party with Ramsay MacDonald at its head. He was first and foremost an orator, displaying the pulpit eloquence lacking in his unpolished trade-union colleagues. Impatient and intransigent, in 1908, only a year after his election, he created two scenes in the House during debates on the licensing laws (throughout which he was himself somewhat the worse for wear through drink).

In 1910 a general election was brewing, and Grayson's poor parliamentary record was brought to light, including the fact that in the previous year he had made just one speech in the House. As with many by-election winners he lost his seat in the general election; but it was another close run thing, the Liberal candidate's radical ticket seducing many of Grayson's supporters. Victor's parliamentary days were over. A later attempt to gain re-election at Kennington in south London proved disastrous.

He threw himself into journalism, although he continued to address political meetings at which the magic of the old oratory was still evident. Through illness, however, he was able to work only periodically; and after his marriage to actress Ruth Nightingale in 1912, he suffered from the extremes of poverty and deprivation on a level which shocked even his old trade-union friends who had witnessed poverty enough in their own lives.

In 1915 Grayson and his wife and newly born daughter emigrated to Australia and subsequently New Zealand where economic prospects seemed a little better. In 1916 he enlisted as a private in the Expeditionary Forces, displaying an impish jingoism curiously at odds with the socialist principle of pacifism. In 1917 he was wounded while serving in France and invalided out of the army suffering from shell-shock. He ended up back in England. A year later his wife died while giving birth to their second child.

Grayson is next to be found living in a prestigious block of flats in London SW1, to which he moved during the course of 1918. Just how this transformation from acute poverty to comparative affluence was achieved is closely bound up with the reasons for his disappearance. Numbered among his friends and regular visitors at this time were the rather unsavoury characters Horatio Bottomley and Maundy Gregory. The former was a Liberal MP. In 1922 he was to be convicted of fraud and sentenced to seven years' imprisonment. The latter acted as a broker in Lloyd George's lucrative honours trade. (When Lloyd George, as Prime Minister, found himself running short of cash to finance his party organization, he bolstered his coffers by selling knight-hoods and peerages to those who could afford to buy them.)

Strangely enough Grayson's actual disappearance was not brought to public attention until seven years after the event, as a result of an article in the *Yorkshire Post*. Information came to light as a result of the interest provoked by the story, and the flow has continued into the present decade.

The most celebrated titbit which surfaced emanated from an old Independent Labour Party MP, Sidney Campion, who in 1939 was working as a journalist. While travelling on the London Underground that year he saw a prosperous-looking Grayson, accompanied by a woman who called him 'Vic', get on the train at Sloane Square. As the train neared Westminster, Campion heard Grayson remark 'Here's the old firm.' Campion subsequently claimed to know a great deal about the circumstances of Grayson's disappearance, alleging that he had died during the Blitz in 1941. Campion himself was later offered the post of public relations officer for the General Post Office by Winston

Churchill. In some way, it was argued, Churchill considered Campion's information dangerous, and well worth the offer of a plum job to suppress.

The second 'definitive' rumour involves the artist George Flemwell, who had apparently been acquainted with Grayson before the First World War. In September 1920 he was painting river scenes on the Thames by Thames Ditton when he espied a motor boat with two men in it making its way towards Ditton Island in the middle of the river. One of the men he recognized as Grayson who, together with his companion, entered a bungalow named Vanity Fair on the island. Flemwell managed to get over to the island and knocked on the door, to be greeted by a woman who denied all knowledge of Grayson. Flemwell had no option but to retire as gracefully as the circumstances permitted. He soon returned to Switzerland where he was living and the story remained untold for many years. It certainly has possibilities, for Vanity Fair belonged to none other than Maundy Gregory.

A later gem surfaced as late as 1970. A man called Smallwood claimed to have met, in 1948, someone living in the vicinity of Mount Pleasant in London, a man who called himself Victor Garston. 'Garston' claimed to have married an actress who died in childbirth, to have emigrated to Australia in 1914 and to have served in France during the war, during the course of which he was wounded. He was very acrimonious about MacDonald and the Labour Party and even produced a photograph of himself, accompanied by Horatio Bottomley, making a speech in support of war bonds.

A fourth sighting concerned an old army comrade from Grayson's service days, Reg Ranby. Ranby was in Madrid in 1930 for the world speedway championships when he bumped into Grayson in Madrid's main shopping centre. Upon being greeted, Grayson hurried away, mumbling that Ranby must be mistaken.

In reality there are only two known facts about Victor Grayson's disappearance. The first identifies the time and the venue of the occurrence. It did not happen on a train journey from Liverpool to Hull. Neither, as some writers have suggested, did it occur at a hotel in The Strand with Grayson, in true *Mary Celeste* fashion, leaving a half-finished glass of whisky on a bar counter, although the truth is scarcely less mysterious.

He actually disappeared from his lodgings in Bury Street, London, on a September day in 1920. He was collected by two men and he left with his suitcases, advising his landlady that he would 'be in touch'. This is the last verified sighting of Victor Grayson.

The second known fact concerns his war medals. Like the invalidity war pension to which he was entitled, these remained unclaimed – until 1939, when records show that they were collected from the New Zealand High Commission in London. The only person who could have collected them was Grayson himself. So he was alive in 1939 – and in London – but what had he been doing for the preceding 20 years?

The answer must lie in his connections with Maundy Gregory. In 1933 Gregory was sent to prison for his role in the honours scandal. As a reward for keeping his mouth shut he was given, on his release, a pension of £2,000 a year and went to live in France. Could Grayson have been aware of the honours scandal at an earlier date and have threatened to expose the affair? This would explain the regular payments being made to him and the rapid improvement in his lifestyle. But a decade later it was considered necessary to send Gregory to France to ensure his silence. It may have become just as necessary to persuade Grayson to emigrate. He had remained a heavy drinker and when he imbibed too freely he didn't know what he was saying or doing. He was much too big a risk to keep in London. And so he was sent away. Like Gregory, he may have gone to France. Over the years there were several sightings of him in Kent – quite convenient for the Dover crossing.

One tempting footnote remains. It was rumoured among his former socialist colleagues that Grayson was the illegitimate offspring of a titled gentleman. His full name was Albert Victor Grayson, and 'Albert Victor' was the name of the Duke of Clarence. Perhaps the coincidence was not unintentional, so to speak. Again, on her deathbed his mother kept saying, over and over, 'the Marlboroughs', the implication being that the Churchill family may have been involved in Victor's heritage (it will be remembered that it was Churchill himself who had offered Sidney Campion the PRO job at the GPO). Such stories have a habit of attaching themselves to the young and the talented.

John Stonehouse

Born in Southampton in 1925, John Stonehouse was brought up between the twin pillars of the co-operative movement and trade unionism to which his mother and father were respectively committed. He narrowly avoided being apprenticed to a butcher and became, instead, a junior clerk in Southampton's probation service, progressing to more responsible work as a result of a manpower shortage. In 1944 he joined the RAF, the most glamorous of the services. On demobilization he studied at the London School of Economics under the tutelage of Harold Laski. Intent upon a political career by this time, he contested unsuccessfully both the 1950 and 1951 general elections, the former in the Conservative bastion of Twickenham and the latter at Burton.

Following a narrow defeat at Burton he was advised by one of the Labour movement's elder statesmen, Fenner Brockway (a colleague of Victor Grayson), to go to Africa and make a name for himself – which he promptly did, working for the Federation of Uganda African Farmers. In an attempt to use this organization as a basis for the development of a politically active co-operative movement, he succeeded in arousing the suspicions of the Colonial Service, which had yet to experience the chill wind of change.

On his return to England the idealist was finally returned to the House of Commons as Labour member for Wednesbury, a town in the west Midlands he described as 'a grimy industrial place, producing car components, nuts, bolts and locks'.

Two years later, in 1959, he was back in Africa – this time in his capacity as an MP – and made the headlines for being deported from Rhodesia for having antagonized the ultra-sensitive administration by making political speeches prior to an election. He may have been saying the right things but he had already developed an uncanny knack of saying them at the wrong time. (A further instance involved his 1960 visit to Kenya, where he campaigned for the release of Mau-Mau terrorists.)

In 1964 the first Labour government for 13 years came to power. Harold Wilson, the youngest prime minister of the twentieth century, appointed the dynamic young member for Wednesbury to the post of Parliamentary Secretary to Roy

Jenkins, Minister of Aviation. Stonehouse launched himself implacably into the task of imposing state controls on the aviation industry – that most competitive of free markets and a cornerstone on which even the most Conservative ministers have come to grief. In the process he became embroiled, rather unwisely, with such flamboyant figures as the arms dealer Geoffrey Edwardes and the independent airline operator Freddie Laker. More ominously he also became involved with the Czechs in his efforts to sell VC-10s to the Czech airline CSA. He also found time to enter the lists in the controversy over the building of Concorde.

Nevertheless his star continued to rise and he was soon elevated to the rank of Privy Councillor, the traditional pomp and circumstance of the appointment holding a strange appeal for the champion of the underdog, the product of parochial trade-unionism. The ultimate accolade came in 1968, however, with his appointment as the last of Britain's Postmasters-General, in which office it fell to him to implement the wide-ranging reforms instigated by his predecessor, Anthony Wedgwood Benn, including the launch of the Giro Bank, two-tier post and the postcode system. He made no secret of his dislike of the task. If he distrusted someone it was not in the new minister's nature to hide the fact, and his antagonism towards Wedgwood Benn, then a powerful figure in the Labour Party, proved no exception. His dislike of Harold Wilson's secretary, Marcia Williams, and the power she wielded at Number 10 was also apparent. This unfortunate lack of diplomacy was to cost him dear, as influential friends were to be sadly lacking in his hour of need.

The first major blow to his prospects occurred in the year of his appointment as Postmaster-General, when a Czech intelligence officer defected to the West. In his efforts to oblige his new friends during the de-briefing process the man named Stonehouse as an informant, working for the Czech Secret Service. This claim was false, but the fact that it had been made at all was sufficient to do irreparable damage. Stonehouse had certainly always been very friendly with the Czechs. Shortly after his election he had visited Prague and, rather naively, had responded warmly to overtures of friendship eagerly proferred by the Czech Embassy in London. Clearly the Czechs had marked him down as a good prospect and he showed no inclination to discourage their attentions, with visits to Leipzig trade fairs, attendances at Czech Embassy cocktail parties, and even managing to arrange for his Wednesbury constituency to be twinned with the Czech town of Kladno. He knew what the Czechs were after, yet he was unable to bring himself to sever his contacts with them.

Stonehouse was grilled about his Czech connections by counter-intelligence. Although it seems unlikely that MI6 believed him guilty of a breach of security, they deemed it prudent to warn him of the dangers of over-fraternization with Eastern bloc officials. He was cleared of the charges.

Early in 1970 the Labour government was defeated at the polls and Stonehouse was deprived not only of ministerial responsibility but also, as a direct result of the Czech incident, of the confidence of his fellow Labour MPs to an extent which led to his failure to gain a place in the shadow cabinet. His income diminished, he decided to supplement it by promoting British exports and set up a limited liability company for this purpose: Export Promotion and Consultancy Services (EPACS).

His interest in the developing world remained undimmed, and he kept a keen eye on the civil war then raging in East Pakistan and on the atrocities committed by the Pakistan military against the Bengalees. Following the establishment of the Bangladesh Republic he was approached by prominent Bengalees in Britain for help in establishing a bank to provide financial services for Bengalee immigrants, replacing the Pakistani banks they had ceased to trust. A bond of mutual understanding and co-operation between Britain and Bangladesh would also be fostered.

The *Financial Times* reported the intentions of the new venture and, in order to explain the objectives to the immigrant Bengalees, a Bengali prospectus-like news-sheet was prepared in which the bank was described as a 'trust', inviting investment. Considerable criticism ensued. Although several major prospective backers held their ground, it was only by committing his personal and business resources, and by borrowing from other banks, that Stonehouse was able to get the project off the ground. In the process the accounts of EPACS became somewhat entangled.

Despite this heroic rearguard action only some £15,000 of

Bengalee share applications were received. Disaster followed upon disaster when the Fraud Squad demonstrated an investigative interest in the preliminary activities of the bank in relation to the Companies Act, thereby damaging what little Bengalee confidence remained. Although the Director of Public Prosecutions decided that there were insufficient grounds for any prosecution, the strain had taken its toll, both on the bank's prospects and upon Stonehouse himself.

And so it came to pass that John Stonehouse, MP for Wednesbury in Staffordshire, took refuge in the anonymity of one Joe Markham (deceased). In November 1974 he took what was ostensibly a business trip to Florida, clutching two passports: his own, and another in the name of Joe Markham. On his arrival at Miami International Airport he managed to queue up twice at the immigration desk and succeeded in being admitted to the United States by harassed immigration officials as both Stonehouse and Markham.

As Stonehouse he was attempting to negotiate an injection of capital into his London Capital Group to offset the huge loans he had negotiated from other banks to keep London Capital afloat. To his horror the National Bank of Miami displayed little or no interest in the investment opportunity. So he went for a swim in the warm coastal waters.

Leaving his clothes on his hotel verandah he swam out to sea as John Stonehouse and returned as Joe Markham. He changed into a secreted second set of clothes, flew to San Francisco and then, via Hawaii and Sydney, to Melbourne. Once there he transferred his funds, deposited in the name of Markham in the Bank of New South Wales, to the Bank of New Zealand and an account previously opened in the name of Donald Clive Mildoon. He rented an executive apartment and as Mildoon, an identity twice removed from that of Stonehouse, he hoped to relax into anonymity.

But he was already under surveillance. Mildoon, the Bank of New Zealand depositor, had been recognized as Markham, the Bank of New South Wales client. The police suspected a banking fraud scheme and picked him up when, as Mildoon, he arranged to collect mail addressed to Markham. By this time, December 1974, they had identified him as Stonehouse. He was locked up as an illegal immigrant and spent a miserable Christmas in isolation. His wife flew out to join him, and this in itself must have been an embarrassment in view of his close relationship with his secretary, Mrs Sheila Buckley. His subsequent fight to remain in Australia proved unsuccessful and he returned to Britain in July 1975 in the care of Scotland Yard detectives, to be temporarily remanded in Brixton prison.

At the time of his disappearance in Florida, John Stonehouse had long since ceased to be headline material. Any British dailies which went so far as to carry the story merely limited themselves to a short paragraph on the inside pages, identifying him as a former postmaster-general. Public appreciation has but a short life-span. Wasn't he that rather nice-looking man who had been involved with the Wilson administration in the 1960s? Some interest was kindled with rumours of suicide or even of Mafia-incited murder. But the wrong questions were being asked. In the absence of a corpse how could anyone be sure he was dead? Such a question came to be considered when it was discovered that, only weeks prior to his disappearance, he had taken out life insurance worth £125,000 to be paid, in the event of his death, to his wife.

The true story behind his disappearance, when it surfaced, had everything a newshound could desire, involving as it did a public figure fallen from grace, a scandal concerning the mis-appropriation of funds, and even an extra-marital love affair. Stonehouse himself saw the issue facing him as a straight contest between unsubstantiated claims that he had stolen £800,000 from the Bangladesh Fund and his own claim that he had not been responsible for his actions.

Although his defence was not one of insanity he gave a fairly good impression of said state of mind in shifting his allegiance as an MP from the Labour Party to the Sunshine Party, a harmless band of assorted crackpots. He put the blame for his actions upon the pressures of public life which had led, he asserted, to the formation within him of multiple personalities (ie Markham and Mildoon).

The prosecution viewed his actions rather less charitably, drawing attention to his creation of 24 bank accounts in no less than 17 different banks, the sums on deposit finding their way to Switzerland, where they were enshrouded in Swiss banking secrecy and lost to investigators. Clearly a considerable degree of skill and cunning had contributed to Stonehouse's efforts to make a new life for himself, and he was sentenced to seven years' imprisonment.

On his release he entertained ambitions to regain political power, but it was not long before he had to come to terms with living out the remainder of his life in obscurity. He died in April 1988, a sick and broken man.

Harold Holt

When John Stonehouse MP arranged his disappearance in Miami in 1974 it is likely that his plans were based on the circumstances surrounding the disappearance, some seven years earlier, of the Australian Premier Harold Holt who, on 17 December 1967, walked into the sea at Portsea, Victoria, and vanished beneath the waves. Holt's own disappearance is, if anything, even more intriguing – and certainly more mystifying – than that of the MP for Wednesbury.

Harold Edward Holt was born in 1908 of theatrical parents. A public school education was followed by three years spent studying law at Queen's College, Melbourne. During his time at university he cultivated a playboy image and, more important, acquired left-wing tendencies which led him to reject Australia's traditional relationship with Britain in favour of closer ties with Asia, notably China. In a paper presented to the university debating society in July 1929, Holt set out the philosophy which would form the cornerstone of his foreign policy in later years, drawing attention to the enormous potential of Asia as a market for Australian manufactured goods. The tone of the paper leaves one in little doubt that in any relationship between the two continents, Australia would be the senior, exploiting partner.

On leaving Melbourne he set up as a lawyer, and in 1931 his star really went into the ascendant when he was introduced to Robert Menzies, destined to become Australia's longest-serving premier, but at that time serving as deputy to Prime Minister Joe Lyons. Keeping his radical opinions in check, Holt was encouraged by his mentor, Menzies, to stand for Parliament as a Liberal, winning a seat (Fawkner) at his second attempt in September 1935.

In 1939 Holt retained Fawkner at the general election and the new Prime Minister, Menzies, immediately appointed him Minister without Portfolio to the Ministry of Supply and Development, followed by the additional appointment of Acting Minister for Air and Civil Aviation – both key posts in the weeks following Australia's entry to the Second World War. However, in March 1940 the government was forced to take to the hustings again and, with a majority of one, Menzies had little option but

Victor Grayson, the socialist MP for Colne Valley, speaking at a demonstration on unemployment on Tower Hill, London in 1909. Grayson's parliamentary career was brief, but his connection with various unsavoury political figures and his sudden rise from extreme poverty to affluence during the First World War has led to speculation that his subsequent disappearance might have been connected with a suppressed political scandal.

Harold Holt, the Australian Prime Minister, was lost beneath the waves while swimming near his holiday home at Portsea, Victoria in December 1967. Holt, who was considered an expert swimmer, is seen above in his skin-diving outfit with the wives of his three step-sons.
The circumstances in which Holt vanished may have influenced John Stonehouse, the former Labour cabinet minister (*left*), when he staged his own disappearance seven years later, swimming out to sea from a Florida beach and returning to shore under the assumed identity of Joe Markham.

left: The master of the *Mary Celeste*, Captain Benjamin Briggs, who disappeared, along with all the passengers and crew, during a voyage from New York to Genoa in November 1872, in perhaps the most celebrated mystery of all time.
below: The *Mary Celeste* in 1861, when she was called the *Amazon*.

to form a coalition. Holt had to return to the back benches to free ministerial posts for leading opposition party members.

He promptly joined the army as a private but, even before his training was over, three government ministers were killed in an air crash and Holt was invited back as Minister of Labour and National Service. Two years afterwards the coalition government collapsed and the Liberals moved over to the Opposition benches where they, and Holt, languished for the next eight years. Holt's frustration was relieved by his marriage during this period to his former university sweetheart Zara, who brought with her three sons by a failed first marriage.

In 1949 the political pendulum swung back to the Liberals and, in power once more, Menzies appointed Holt as Minister of Labour and Minister for Immigration. In due course he was made deputy leader of the Liberal Party and Leader of the House. In the mid-1950s he also acquired a holiday home at Portsea and became a keen skin-diver. Later in the decade he became Federal Treasurer, a post to which he did not feel naturally suited but which was regarded as a significant stepping-stone on his way to the premiership.

His moment came in 1966 when Menzies finally decided to hand over the reins of power to a younger man. Holt loved the publicity that came with the job of prime minister. It was shortly after he took over that the famous photograph of Holt in skin-diving suit, flanked by the three glamorous, scantily clad wives of his step-sons, was taken. The process of government was not quite so attractive.

Holt was committed to Australian involvement in the Vietnam War – he himself had been responsible for introducing national service after the Second World War – and he now became the object of much maternal wrath from the mothers whose sons made up the planned 3,000-man Australian contribution to the US war effort. In effect Australia had merely exchanged one master (Britain) for another (America), and it was now President Lyndon Johnson who called the tune.

The Liberals, with Holt at the helm, continued to enjoy the same broadly-based level of support they had commanded in Menzies' day and romped home in the landslide general election victory of November 1966. But if Holt was still something of a charismatic figure as far as the electorate was concerned, he was becoming an increasingly difficult colleague with whom to work. He had always shown a marked personal preference for involvement in foreign affairs at the expense of domestic matters – a tendency which grew more pronounced as time went on. He did not seem to have the capacity to weather run-of-the-mill attacks by the Opposition. He had been accused of allowing VIP aircraft to be used for his friends and his family; he had committed an astonishing elementary breach of protocol in Parliament by rudely interrupting a new member's maiden speech; he was under continuous pressure from the Americans to increase the number of Australian troops in Vietnam at a time of growing disenchantment with the war among Australians.

Holt's weekend breaks at his Portsea home were becoming more and more valuable to him as a means of 'switching off' when the pressures of high public office threatened to overwhelm him. The weekend of 15–17 December 1967 promised to be no different to any other, except that his wife remained in Melbourne to make preparations for Christmas, so that he was accompanied only by their housekeeper. For much of the weekend he enjoyed his usual hectic social round. His activities included a strenuous game of tennis, though his performance was below par due to a shoulder problem. On the morning of 17 December with a select group of companions, he visited Cheviot Beach for a swim.

Cheviot Beach enjoyed a reputation as one of the most dangerous in Victoria, dotted with lethal rocks and swept by a raging surf. On that Sunday morning the water was exceptionally turbulent. Unperturbed, Holt swam out to sea. Only one of his companions, a much younger man, Alan Stewart, dared venture near the water and, although he kept within his depth, he could still feel strong undercurrents dragging at his heels. Suddenly, Holt appeared to be engulfed by heavy turbulence and disappeared from view. A quickly organized air-sea search failed to find any trace of the prime minister, dead or alive.

It had all been a tragic accident. Over-confident and partially incapacitated, Holt had swum too far out in a turbulent sea. Unable to handle the deadly undercurrents, he had been pulled under and drowned, his body probably being swept out into the ocean.

But there were those who did not subscribe to the accident theory. Perhaps, depressed by his political problems, he had committed suicide? Perhaps he had been assassinated by frog-men lying in wait for him? There were, it is true, some minor unusual aspects to the incident. For example, Holt had been without a bodyguard that day, which seemed odd in view of the fact that security had been stepped up following an attack upon the Labour leader, Arthur Calwell. Yet Holt was well known for wandering off alone. He had been doing it for years and, even had a security man been assigned to him, it is probable that Holt would have succeeded in giving him the slip.

Again, subsequent incidents in the area, although doubtless unrelated to Holt's disappearance, took on new meaning by virtue of their tenuous connections with Cheviot Beach. On 20 December 1967, three days after Holt's disappearance, his swimming companion, Alan Stewart, was involved in a car crash. Was someone trying to stop him from 'talking'? In November 1974 a retired army officer called Brown went missing in the vicinity of Cheviot Beach while walking his dog. According to local gossip Brown had always been suspicious of the circum-stances of Holt's disappearance. Had he been silenced? If so, why had 'they' waited seven years to do it?

By far the most sensational alternative explanation for Holt's disappearance was provided by the distinguished British journalist Anthony Grey. His book *The Prime Minister Was A Spy*, published in 1983, proposed the case that Holt was spying for China (in view of his Asian sympathies) and that he had been doing so continuously since his university days, communicating with his masters in Peking by means of an obtuse code used in the voluminous correspondence he kept up with friends and relatives during his frequent globe-trotting trips. Frightened lest his cover was about to be blown, he had asked the Chinese to stage a rescue mission. Far from drowning, he had been pulled down by frogmen, provided with breathing apparatus and taken to a waiting Chinese submarine (after which point in time, his movements remain unknown).

This mind-boggling tale was allegedly retailed to Grey by a mysterious Australian businessman who wished, not surpris-ingly, to preserve his anonymity. Unfortunately there is not a shred of evidence to support his claims. Harold Holt was a strong swimmer. He was well acquainted with Cheviot Beach. But here, as in his political life, the tide had turned against him.

6

THE *MARY CELESTE*

If one were to be asked to identify the most mysterious disappearance of all time, the chances are that the case of the *Mary Celeste* would spring to mind. The very name is synonymous with mystery and the supernatural. Even those with little or no interest at all in the subject generally are acquainted with this intriguing tale of the inexplicable. Strangely enough, very little of substance has been written about the *Mary Celeste*, fact and fiction having become inextricably intertwined in a labyrinth of inaccurate magazine and newspaper articles, calculated to perpetuate a mystery as opposed to proferring likely explanations.

The *Mary Celeste* began life in 1861 as *The Amazon*, a brigantine of around 200 tons. Following an early career of mishaps she was refitted and renamed *Mary Celeste* in 1869. Three years later in October 1872, Benjamin Briggs was appointed captain, acquiring, after the fashion of the times, a part-share in the vessel.

On 5 November 1872 the *Mary Celeste* set out on her fateful voyage from Pier 50 on New York's East River. It was a premature start, for, due to bad weather, she had to put into Staten Island almost immediately, leaving there two days later, bound for Genoa with a cargo of raw alcohol. She was not sighted again until 5 December. At approximately 1300 hours on that day Captain David Morehouse, master of the *Dei Gratia*, a vessel of similar proportions to the *Mary Celeste*, espied her at a point about 500 miles east of the Azores. Morehouse was a good friend of Briggs. They had dined together on the eve of Briggs's departure from New York, the *Dei Gratia* having embarked on 15 November en route for Gibraltar with a cargo of petroleum.

It was with some concern that Morehouse observed the *Mary Celeste*'s silent and empty decks. A small boarding party was

68

dispatched from the *Dei Gratia* and it was soon discovered that there was, indeed, not a soul on board. Furthermore, it seemed that the vessel had been abandoned in considerable haste. The brig's charts and even her log (completed up to 24 November) were still aboard. There was even an imprint of a child's body on an unmade bed. Although the chronometer, sextant and the ship's papers were missing, there were two peculiarities which were to lead to much surmise at a later date: under the captain's bunk was discovered what appeared to be a bloodstained sword; and on the port bow, about three feet above the water line, a long narrow strip of the edge of one of the vessel's outer planks was cut away to a depth of about three-eighths of an inch for a length of about six feet. In addition it was noted that there were three and a half feet of water in the hold. On the cabin table was a slate on which had been hurriedly scribbled: 'Fanny my dear wife. Frances M R.'

Morehouse seconded three of his own crew to the drifting derelict and set sail for Gibraltar. In so doing his motives were not entirely altruistic. The *Mary Celeste* was a considerable prize as far as salvage value was concerned. Whatever the case the derelict, with her makeshift crew, docked in Gibraltar on (appropriately enough) Friday 13 December. Five days later a court of enquiry was convened.

An official survey showed that the *Mary Celeste* was seaworthy and failed to find any evidence of structural damage. However, the Attorney-General of Gibraltar, Solly Flood, made much of the bloodstained sword (which, on examination, proved to be merely rusty) and the cuts on the vessel's bows, together with the fact that one barrel of the raw alcohol appeared to have been tampered with. He made no secret of his personal view that the crew had become inebriated through drinking the alcohol and, having murdered Briggs and his wife and child, who had accompanied him on the voyage, made good their escape in one of the longboats. For indulging in this line of reasoning Flood has been much maligned. But what other likely explanation could there be?

It was also suggested, in a similarly uncharitable fashion, that the incident was part of a scheme in which Briggs, his co-owners and Morehouse were involved, to defraud the insurers. Doubtless such suspicions were uppermost in Admiralty minds when

Morehouse and his crew were awarded a salvage cheque for less than £2,000 – a tidy sum in those times but only a fifth of the total amount to which Morehouse felt he was entitled. No definitive reason for the abandonment of the *Mary Celeste* was proposed and the event became another mystery to be blamed on the vagaries of the Atlantic Ocean.

It was hoped, of course, that evidence in the form of bodies might come to light at a future date. Before the days of steam and wireless the major sea-lanes of the world were peppered with drifting lifeboats crammed with decayed corpses. No such grisly finds, however, could be linked with the mystery of the *Mary Celeste*.

Ten years elapsed and, but for the efforts of one man, the story might have sunk into oblivion. Then, in 1884, the January issue of the *Cornhill* magazine rekindled the dying embers of the old controversy with a feature entitled 'J. Habakuk Jephson's Statement'. Jephson claimed to be a survivor of the tragedy, one of three passengers on the vessel. Another passenger, Septimus Goring, apparently murdered the captain and crew so that he could take the ship to Africa. Jephson, luckier than the others, was set adrift in a boat from which he was subsequently rescued.

This tale was believed by many to be true – not surprisingly, for it came from the pen of no less an author than Sir Arthur Conan Doyle. It was pure fiction and carries the hallmarks of much of Conan Doyle's work – certainly in respect of the larger-than-life names of the central characters. Like his contemporary, the mystery writer Arthur Machen, Conan Doyle possessed the gift of being able to present his fiction in such a way that it came, by many of his readers, to be accepted as fact. Even his faux pas in naming the vessel the '*Marie Celeste*' stuck, so that to this day we speak of the '*Marie Celeste*' as opposed to the '*Mary Celeste*'.

'Survivor' stories have a special attraction, appealing to the instinct for adventure which lies unnourished inside us all. Such yarns are invariably accepted as factual. Thomas Berger's novel *Little Big Man*, made into a successful film starring Dustin Hoffman and purporting to be the autobiography of a survivor of Custer's Last Stand, has on more than one occasion been recommended as a factual portrayal. One is unsure whether this is a compliment to the author's skills or testimony to human gullibility.

The case of the *Mary Celeste* was no exception. Taking Conan Doyle's story as a lead, several claimants for the title 'sole survivor of the world's most mysterious maritime disappearance' broke into print. In 1913, for instance, the *Strand* magazine (which had published most of the classic Sherlock Holmes short stories) carried a stirring tale by an apparently reputable scholar, Howard Linford, concerning a collection of papers bequeathed to him by an old servant, Abel Fosdyke.

Allegedly a member of the ship's crew, Fosdyke told a most remarkable story. During her fatal voyage Captain Briggs, unable to cope with considerable rough weather, suffered something in the nature of a nervous breakdown. During a subsequent period of calm, he and the mate indulged in the curious pastime of a swimming race around the ship. Mrs Briggs and her baby, together with the crew, were watching from the quarterdeck, which collapsed under their weight and pitched them into the sea. All save Fosdyke were gobbled up by sharks. Clinging to the floating quarterdeck he was ultimately washed up on the coast of North Africa.

An even more farcical account appeared in the July 1926 edition of *Chambers Journal*. This time the author's informant was John Pemberton, a 92-year-old former ship's cook residing at the port of Liverpool. Pemberton described a scenario in which the *Mary Celeste* was embroiled in a hurricane with the captain and crew fighting and bickering among themselves. During a spell of fine weather Mrs Briggs was playing the piano when a sudden squall turned the ship on its end. The unfortunate lady (who, according to Pemberton, was of such diminutive stature as to be dwarf-like) was crushed against the wall behind the piano, having slid across the cabin floor from one end to the other. The first mate threw the piano overboard, but Captain Briggs refused to do the same with his dead wife. The mate insisted and Briggs, insane with grief, jumped over the side after her. Mortal fights on board further reduced the number of crew. Sighted by the *Dei Gratia* the remaining crew reached an agreement with Captain Morehouse by which the *Mary Celeste* was to be taken in tow to Gibraltar as a derelict with a view to claiming the salvage money.

The *Nautical Magazine* of December 1913 produced a Greek sailor who claimed to have survived the tragedy. Demetrius

Specioti maintained that, in approaching Gibraltar, the *Mary Celeste* was met by another vessel which turned out to be full of pirates. The *Mary Celeste*'s crew were put to work on the pirate ship. After many trials and tribulations, the end result of which was that the *Mary Celeste* men overpowered the pirates, the craft was in collision with an ocean liner, Specioti being the sole survivor of the consequent wreck.

Despite the stirring fare on offer, all the survivor stories can be safely discounted, if for no other reason than none of the claimants – if they ever existed – belonged to the stricken crew. The entire complement comprised Captain Briggs, his wife and baby daughter, two American-born mates, an American cook and four German seamen. Seafaring men were (and still are) notoriously superstitious, and it is one of the minor (and usually ignored) mysteries of the case as to why none of the crew appeared to mind setting sail with a woman on board – one of the unluckiest ways to start a merchant voyage.

Many attempts have been made to discredit the crew – especially the German contingent – and to argue that mutiny is the most likely explanation for the abandonment of the vessel. According to the precious little information we have to hand, the crew, without exception, appear to have been sober and level-headed, although that is not to say that some of the more dramatic accounts questioning their loyalty can be summarily discounted.

For example, is it possible that Captain Briggs, in a spiritual frenzy, slaughtered the whole crew and then jumped into the sea? Incredible as it may seem, there is on record at least one instance in which this actually happened. It concerns the *Mary Russell* en route to Cork, having sailed from Barbados in May 1828. On board were Captain William Stewart, six men, three boys and four passengers. Early in the voyage Stewart began suffering delusions that the crew were plotting to murder him. With the aid of the ingenuous youths, his pistols, a harpoon and an axe, he systematically butchered eight of the men on board. He thought he had killed the remaining two and was about to start on the boys when another ship drew alongside. During the remainder of the voyage to Ireland, Stewart threw himself overboard. Subsequent apprehension led to his incarceration in an asylum for the remaining 20 years of his life. With one or two minor variations this sequence of events could very easily apply to the *Mary Celeste*.

A similar horrific tale concerned the *Veronica*, which left Mexico for Montivideo in October 1902. One of the crew, a German, Gustav Rau, incited the crew to mutiny. Having brutally murdered everyone else on board, Rau and three companions fired the ship and took to a lifeboat. But for the fact that one of the mutineers broke down and told the truth of what had happened, the world would have been no wiser. Had they not been picked up at all, there would have been no clue whatsoever. The *Veronica* would simply have become another statistic in the records of vanishing ships.

Truth is often stranger than fiction, and we would do well to bear this in mind when being tempted to dismiss this or that theory as too fantastic. Evidence often dismissed in this way is that provided by Spiritualists. At a seance in California, Mrs Briggs was contacted through a medium. The spirit of the captain's wife confirmed that she did, in fact, play her piano while on board. Whenever she played, she said, faint music could be heard as if in response to her own playing. At a point to the east of the Azores, Captain Briggs thought that the vessel was passing over what had been the continent of Atlantis and, strangely enough, the *Mary Celeste* ran aground on an unknown shore, which Briggs believed to be the lost continent risen miraculously from the sea. As soon as everyone was ashore the island sank beneath them and all were drowned. The *Mary Celeste*, however, merely drifted off and continued on her way.

A further possibility is that the entire crew could have suffered from ergot poisoning, a ghastly complaint from which we no longer have any fears. It concerns a fungus which adheres to rye – rendering both beer and bread susceptible – and which formerly could lead to negative LSD-type hallucinations, with attendant madness and suicide. There are on record many well-documented cases of the appalling effects of ergot poisoning on entire communities, down to and including the early years of this century.

By far the most likely option, and the explanation most favoured by investigators, is that in a moment of ill-founded panic the *Mary Celeste* was abandoned, and the crew, for some reason, were unable to return to her when it became apparent that the decision to leave had been unsound. A decision to abandon ship could have been taken for one of three reasons. The first, and least likely, would have been on the grounds of inclement weather. Briggs was an experienced seaman. Dealing with rough weather – and aboard a brigantine in the North Atlantic the weather could make life very unpleasant – was his business. If the *Mary Celeste* had been fighting a losing battle against a storm of worse than usual proportions, there would have been a period of time for captain and crew to make arrangements for a more orderly departure than was the case. What we need in order to explain the mystery is an incident which would have instilled panic into the crew and which, in turn, would have led to the hasty departure clearly indicated. There are two possibilities.

The explanation most favoured by investigators concerns the three and a half feet of water in the hold. Having been through heavy storms, Briggs ordered a member of the crew to sound the pumps. Finding a quantity of water in the pumps at that moment and misreading the depth, the crewman panicked, gave the alarm and the vessel was abandoned. This is an unlikely story because Briggs was an experienced master. It is difficult to see him abandoning ship through such a fundamental error.

The second possibility involves the nature of the cargo: commercial alcohol. As one of the 1,701 barrels of alcohol had been found opened, it seemed possible, in the first instance, that the crew may have got drunk on the contents and mutinied under the influence. Detractors of this theory point out that commercial alcohol is not at all palatable. Neither, one may rejoin, is methylated spirits but desperate individuals do drink it. Be that as it may, there is another angle from which to approach the problem of the split cask.

Although undrinkable as far as refined tastes are concerned, raw alcohol is exceptionally volatile and under certain conditions liable to explode. Although there was no trace of an explosion on board, the cargo may have begun to rumble – as raw alcohol will do prior to exploding – and caused the crew, in mortal fear of being blown out of the water, to abandon ship.

There are, on record, examples of ships being abandoned because of both miscalculated soundings and fear of explosion. For example, in 1919 the *Marion C. Douglas* was abandoned by her crew off Newfoundland because they believed, quite erroneously, that she was sinking. Similarly, Captain Cook's *Endeavour* was almost abandoned in 1768 when, off the Australian coast, soundings were taken and the depth misread.

Captain Winchester, part-owner of the *Mary Celeste*, recollected hearing a story from an old sea captain about alcohol exploding at sea. His informant described an explosion in the main hatch, from which burst forth steam and smoke. Coming to the conclusion that the ship was on fire the crew lowered the longboat and clambered on to it. As the captain was about to follow suit he turned to look at the hatch and noticed that the smoke had ceased. On checking further he found no trace of fire in the hold and no indication that any explosion of greater magnitude was likely to occur. Accordingly the vessel proceeded on her way.

In choosing between the two theories it must be borne in mind that the *Mary Celeste* was nearing the end of her voyage, having successfully traversed more than 2,000 miles of ocean. Although the ship's log had been completed up to only 24 November, the slate which contained the words 'Fanny my dear wife. Frances M R' also bore notes relating to an observation made at 8am on 25 November. This gave the *Mary Celeste*'s position as just six miles from Santa Maria Island in the Azores. Only a danger of the greatest magnitude, sudden and in all probability unexpected, could lead an experienced master mariner to abandon his vessel – and, we must remember, his livelihood – to the mercy of the Atlantic. The fear of an impending explosion would be the only realistic reason for him to do so.

Although this probability may solve the problem of why the vessel was abandoned, it still leaves the riddle of the crew's disappearance. If, as seems certain, they abandoned ship successfully in a longboat, what was their ultimate fate? When encountered by the *Dei Gratia*, the *Mary Celeste* was almost 400 miles east of the Azores and 600 miles from Gibraltar, but at the time of her abandonment, taking into account the information contained in her log, she must still have been comparatively close to the Azores.

In the earlier quoted case of the *Veronica* mutineers, the rebellious seaman Gustav Rau and his companions scuttled the ship in mid-ocean with Rau, an ordinary seaman, steering their small boat to the safety of the Brazilian coast. There is also the epic voyage of Captain Bligh, cast adrift from the *Bounty* in the Pacific in 1789, who navigated a longboat over 3,000 miles to Java. Not to put too fine a point on it, the task facing Captain Briggs and his companions was quite a simple one, particularly as, despite their hurried departure, they had managed to take the ship's navigational instruments with them. It is also likely that a tow rope would have been attached to the *Mary Celeste*, although if there had been danger of an explosion it is possible that this standard safety procedure would have been deliberately neglected.

Relief at getting clear of the vessel they feared was about to be destroyed must be balanced against the horror that all must have felt as they saw her, unscathed, drift off towards the horizon. Instead of making for the safety of the Azores, did Briggs make the fatal mistake of attempting to catch her, hoping against hope for a period of calm, or perhaps a favourable wind which might turn her about – and, in so doing, consign himself and his companions to an agonizing death and a watery grave?

The *Mary Celeste* herself lived on. She was kept in Gibraltar for three months while the court of enquiry deliberated, after which she was permitted to complete her voyage to Genoa, which she accomplished successfully on 21 March 1873. Following a short spell in dry dock she returned to the United States, reaching New York in the month of September.

During the course of the next seven years she changed ownership, and part-owners, several times until in February 1880 she came into the possession of a consortium headed by Mr Wesley Grove. Eleven months later she met her end on reefs off Haiti, on which occasion she was carrying a cargo of beer. This time there was clear evidence of a scheme to defraud her insurers.

It was discovered that each beer barrel was listed as containing more beer than it could possibly hold. Further investigation showed that the beer was in fact water. Additional cargo was found to have been misrepresented in a similar fashion and the vessel's master, Captain Gilman Parker, was charged with conspiracy and the wilful wrecking of his ship.

During the course of the trial it came to light that the reef struck by the *Mary Celeste* was both clearly marked on her charts and clearly visible at the time. It had also been a clear day with calm waters. In fact the hapless crewman at the wheel had been ordered to steer straight for the reef.

The grossly over-insured value of the worthless cargo was £25,000, on which basis claims had been made and actually paid. Strangely enough the trial jury failed to agree on a verdict. Considering the incontrovertible mass of evidence to the contrary, it is difficult to appreciate how any fair-minded (and unbribed) juror could suggest that Captain Parker was innocent of the charges laid against him.

Before a new trial could be arranged, Parker died, as did his first mate. All the companies involved in the fraud collapsed, one of their proprietors going so far as to commit suicide. This unfortunate turn of affairs has lent weight to the arguments of those who see the *Mary Celeste* as a jinxed ship, although there is little mystery in the ultimate failure of a number of shady business undertakings, or in the suicide of one who gambled on the success of a fraud and lost.

The story of the *Mary Celeste* is a strange mixture of fact, fraud and fantasy. The fraud is explicit enough. The fantasies are many: the longboats slung on their davits; the half-eaten, hurriedly abandoned breakfast in the captain's cabin; the open and unspilled bottle of cough medicine standing upright on a narrow shelf. The facts surrounding the crew's abandonment of the vessel will always remain a matter for conjecture. One thing we know for certain. Whatever caused them to forsake the safety of their vessel, it cannot have instilled in them a greater sense of horror than they must have felt as they watched the still seaworthy *Mary Celeste* sail unmanned before them, capriciously, tauntingly, always keeping out of reach – leading them on to the open sea – almost as if, might one say, she had a mind of her own?

7

THE LOST PATROL

Second only to the *Mary Celeste* in the annals of mysterious disappearances is the notorious area of the western Atlantic, off the south-east coast of the United States, known as the Bermuda Triangle. The number of past and continuing inexplicable disappearances of ships in its waters and aircraft in the skies above is of such magnitude that the theme has never become hackneyed. Each author who approaches the subject afresh has a wealth of new material with which to illustrate his arguments.

It often surprises people to learn that the concept of the Bermuda Triangle is quite a new one. It was first popularized on a large scale by the American author Charles Berlitz (of phrase book and language guide fame) who went straight into the bestseller lists in 1975 with his book *The Bermuda Triangle*, which has sold more than five million copies. Berlitz's book was not the first. In 1973 Adi-Kent Thomas Jeffrey had published a book of the same title. In 1974 Richard Winer produced *The Devil's Triangle* and as far back as 1969 John Wallace Spencer had written *Limbo of the Lost*. None of these offerings, however, quite caught on in the way Berlitz's study did, and it must have proved a depressing experience for the earlier authors. It remains one of the greatest mysteries of the Bermuda Triangle.

The person most entitled to be chagrined is a writer called Vincent Gaddis, who can be credited with laying the foundations of the Bermuda Triangle legend with an article which appeared in the American magazine *Argosy* in 1964. The article told of the mysterious disappearance of no less than five US Navy torpedo bombers off the Florida coast in December 1945. This case has become the cornerstone of the legend around which the many hundreds of other disappearances, before and since, cling with limpet-like tenacity. It is the disappearance of Flight 19 which

78

provides cohesion to the very concept of an area of ocean in and over which an unusually high level of disappearances are concentrated.

Flight 19 was a training flight. The trainees were based at Fort Lauderdale, Florida, a demobilization centre for veterans of the recently ended war as well as a training centre for prospective veterans of the next one. Flight 19 itself comprised five Avenger torpedo bombers, one of the most powerful and efficient aircraft of its type ever built and in its design far ahead of its time. Each aircraft carried three men: pilot, radio operator and gunner. Not all the participants were trainees. The flight leader, Lieutenant Charles Taylor, was a veteran of pre-war days while others such as Sergeant Robert Gallivan had seen active service throughout the war in the bloody Pacific campaigns. In all there were 14 men. Gunner Corporal Allen Kosnar reported sick, leaving the flight one member short. Kosnar later admitted that he had had a premonition not to fly on that day, 5 December 1945.

At 2pm Flight 19 took off for what was a routine navigational exercise. The mission, involving two hours' flight time, involved an outward run to the Bahamas, where practice bombing runs would be made, followed by a northward turn to Great Sale Cay with a final turn south-west and home: a triangular course within the Bermuda Triangle itself.

At around 3.45pm, shortly before the mission was due to be completed, the control tower at Fort Lauderdale received a frantic call from Lieutenant Taylor to the effect that he was lost. It proved difficult to maintain rational contact with him, and a request to assume a bearing due west was met with the comment 'We don't know which way is west. Everything is wrong. . . . Even the ocean doesn't look as it should.'

This experienced airman then compounded his extraordinary statement by handing over leadership of the flight to a colleague, Captain George Stivers. It was then Stivers' turn to relay a garbled message about being hopelessly lost.

By this time, around 4.30pm, a rescue operation had been launched from the Banana River naval station north of Fort Lauderdale. Lieutenant Harry Cone, with a crew of 12, was heading out to sea in a Martin Mariner flying boat. After giving two position reports this well-equipped sea-plane, bigger than a Flying Fortress bomber, with an experienced crew, vanished.

Nothing more was heard from her.

As for the Avengers, at just after 7pm a barely audible message – the very last one – was picked up. It ran, 'FT . . . FT' which was part of Flight 19's call signal. And then, complete silence. In all, six aircraft and 27 personnel had vanished. At 3.45pm that day everything had seemed normal. By dawn the following day the biggest air-sea search in history was under way, involving hundreds of aircraft and 20 ships and covering an area of nearly 300,000 square miles. It turned up precisely nothing.

The starting point for any investigation of the mysterious events of that December day in 1945 must be the separation of the disappearance of Flight 19 and that of the Mariner rescue vessel. It is far too simple to group together what are two distinctly separate events.

The disappearance of the Mariner is a little easier to explain than that of its quarry. Due to the long distances it had to travel in connection with its air-sea rescue function it was necessary for it to carry an immense amount of fuel – some 2,000 gallons. As a result, these vessels had acquired the nickname of 'flying gas tanks'. It was necessary to take the same precautions that had been taken with the old Zeppelins before the war: prior to each flight the crew had to be searched for matches, cigarette lighters and other personal items which, if used, might cause a spark and, in turn, an explosion. In the event of an emergency (and every call on the services of a Mariner would be an emergency) it is understandable that this procedure might be overlooked.

A cigarette lighter, an electrical fault, a flash of lightning in a heavy, storm-laden atmosphere: any one of these could have sparked off an explosion. That there was an explosion about 50 miles out from the Banana River naval air base in the estimated locality of the sea-plane is certain. An oil tanker, the *Gaines Mills*, reported sighting a ball of flame descending into the ocean at about 8pm. The vessel's master was sure that what he had witnessed was an exploding aeroplane. By the time the *Gaines Mills* reached the exact location all that remained was an oil slick on the surface. Neither wreckage nor bodies were ever found. Although we cannot say beyond all shadow of a doubt that this was the fate of the Mariner sea-plane, it is the most likely explanation in light of all the available information which, it must be admitted, is precious little.

The disappearance of Flight 19 presents us with a very different problem. There is no evidence of any explosion or other extraneous interference with the mission, and the disturbing radio messages sent by Taylor and Stivers add to an unpleasantly eerie scenario, highly unconducive to what might be called a rational solution.

As noted above, the weather at the time was less than satisfactory. It worsened gradually until Flight 19 found itself in a tropical storm. Not that this should have posed any fatal problem in itself – particularly for an experienced flight leader. And Taylor was an experienced pilot, although he had, it is true, never actually flown the exact route on the day's schedule. Although the official enquiry absolved Taylor from any responsibility for the disaster, it must be admitted that his action in handing over command of the flight to Captain Stivers was, to say the least, curious. It has been suggested, quite unfairly, that he had been drinking prior to take-off. He had made a request to be relieved of his flight duty for the day and, like Corporal Kosnar, it may be that he had experienced an unsettling premonition about the flight. When things began to go wrong his powers of judgement could have become clouded, in the belief that his premonition had proved accurate.

One of the most spectacular theories proposed for explaining the tragedy involved UFOs. This was given some impetus by the testimony of a Florida radio ham who had tuned into the transmissions between Taylor and the flight tower. The last message from Taylor that he purported to hear were the words: 'Don't come after me. They look like they're from outer space.' So, had Flight 19 been abducted by a UFO? The idea was developed by Steven Spielberg in *Close Encounters of the Third Kind*. In the film all five Avengers were discovered, in pristine condition, in the desert. At the end Lieutenant Taylor and his colleagues emerged from the flying saucer, looking much the same as they must have done when abducted 30 years before.

A rather more cynical explanation is provided by those who argue that the flight was lost because the crews were engaging in fraudulent activities, deliberately flying off-course in order to extend their flight time and qualify for a flight-pay bonus. To qualify for the payment, pilots had to clock-up six flying hours per month. It is claimed, therefore, that Flight 19 was – initially at least – only simulating orientation problems in order to contribute to the six-hour monthly figure. The Bermuda Triangle is not an area in which many people would choose to play such a dangerous game. Certainly, Taylor's misgivings about flying at all on that day would argue against it.

A decidedly bland interpretation of events was offered by the senior flight instructor at Fort Lauderdale, Lieutenant Robert Cox. His testimony is important because he was in the air himself at the same time as Flight 19 and was able to maintain radio communication with Taylor at an intelligible level for much longer than the Fort Lauderdale control tower. Cox described the loss of the aircraft as 'a chain of unfortunate events and plain human frailty', basing his opinion on an involved series of radio messages which passed back and forth between Taylor and himself.

Cox established contact with Flight 19 while he was encircling the Fort Lauderdale airfield in preparation for landing. This fortuitous occurrence should have been Taylor's passport out of trouble. He indicated that his compasses were not functioning and that he was lost, adding that he appeared to be flying over the Florida Keys. If true, this would have put Flight 19 200 miles off-course to the south-west. Accepting Taylor's estimate of his position, Cox advised him to 'put the sun on your port wing . . . and fly up the coast until you get to Miami. Fort Lauderdale is 20 miles further . . . directly on your left.'

To his credit Cox flew out in an attempt to guide Taylor into port. But instead of being able to maintain radio contact he found the transmissions from Flight 19 becoming fainter and fainter, until they disappeared altogether. Then Cox's own radio failed and he had no option but to return to Fort Lauderdale, where he was denied permission to take up another plane. Through the years Cox steadfastly maintained that he knew exactly where Taylor was. In fact the available evidence suggests that, initially at least, he had no idea.

In accepting Taylor's own estimate of his position as being over the Florida Keys and advising him to fly north, Cox had unwittingly led Taylor into more trouble. Taylor was nowhere near the Florida Keys. He was, in all probability, cruising aimlessly over the Grand Cays, a chain of islands in the Bahamas which, from the air, look remarkably like the Florida Keys.

Without knowing it he was well within the range of the original flight plan, but a course charted to the north simply took him out into the Atlantic Ocean.

To complicate matters even further, as well as maintaining radio contact with both Lieutenant Cox and the Fort Lauderdale control tower, Taylor also started receiving transmissions from the air-sea rescue base at Port Everglades. He informed the base that the flight was at an altitude of 3,500 feet. Little in the way of constructive advice could be given because, incredible as it may seem, there was no direction-finding equipment at Port Everglades. Worse was to follow. Although the Port Everglades personnel were little more than helpless observers, several radio stations had managed to obtain bearings which enabled the position of Flight 19 to be fixed at a point about 150 miles northeast of Fort Lauderdale, well to the north of the Bahamas. Flight 19, however, was not informed, and Taylor continued to labour under the misapprehension that he was much further south. Accordingly he kept changing course – first north, then east, and so on – thinking he was flying into the Gulf of Mexico. Taylor's penultimate message was that all the aircraft were to close up and assume a tight formation so that when the first plane ran out of fuel they would be in a position to ditch together.

When this time eventually arrived, all hope was still not lost. Some have claimed that Avenger aircraft usually sank within seconds of hitting the water. Others argue that the Avenger could remain afloat for up to half an hour. The truth, as usual, may well lie within these extreme estimates. If guided down it seems reasonable to presume that an Avenger might stay afloat for a few minutes – certainly long enough for the crews to launch the life rafts with which they were equipped. Why, then, were no survivors ever found?

Naturally there were many mistaken 'sightings'. There were several instances of jetsam being wrongly identified as life rafts. Other reports mentioned the sighting of distress flares in the Banana River area. One such report came from a Captain Morrison who saw flares and human figures in swampland near Melbourne in Florida on 8 December, three days after the disappearance. Although the sighting was subsequently confirmed, search parties failed to turn anything up. Melbourne is at a point on the Florida coast due west of the radio-fix position obtained on Flight 19. Taylor, as we know, had been flying first north, then east. Had he suddenly set a course due west and reached the coastline? It seems unlikely that he would have had the fuel to do so. And if he had, then his radio transmissions, as he neared the coast, should have gained in strength as opposed to fading away.

Wreckage said to emanate from Flight 19 has been dredged up over the years. In 1961, for example, aircraft wreckage accompanied by human bones was discovered during dredging operations on the Banana River. Examination of the wreckage tended to suggest that it was part of an aircraft other than an Avenger.

Something more promising appeared early in 1987 when a salvage vessel hoisted up the remains of what was definitely an Avenger in the sea, 20 miles to the west of Key West. No human remains were on board the plane, which was found submerged in just 30 feet of water. In some ways the mystery is further compounded. If the remains were those of a Flight 19 Avenger it means that Taylor was correct when he thought he was over the Keys, which makes nonsense of the radio-fix position. We are left with the additional problem of how the crew failed to survive in shallow coastal waters.

Wreckage from crashed aircraft of the Second World War is still turning up all over the world and will doubtless continue to do so for many years to come. More clues as to the ultimate fate of Flight 19 may even be uncovered, but it is unlikely that any light will be shed on the reasons for the disorientation responsible for it.

A disturbingly similar disappearance occurred in June 1974 with the loss of a light plane over the Bahamas. The pilot, Carolyn Cascio, accompanied by one passenger, was on a flight from Nassau to Grand Turk Island. When she reached the spot where Grand Turk Island should have been, she sent a radio message to the effect that she was circling over two unidentified islands which appeared to be unpopulated. It was as though she were flying in a void – almost as if she had entered another dimension. Oddly, airfield personnel on Grand Turk could see the aircraft circling above them, although Cascio was apparently unable to see them. Half an hour later, contact was lost. Had the plane somehow entered another dimension, or even another time, and become 'locked in'?

Other cases of strange flights within the Bermuda Triangle

involve aircraft which seem to have entered an alien dimension, emerging from it with an apparent gain in time. One such case is that of a National Airlines aircraft which, on approaching Miami airport, disappeared from radar tracking control screens. Ten minutes later it just as mysteriously reappeared. No one on board had experienced anything remotely peculiar but, on landing, all watches and clocks were found to be 10 minutes slow even though, according to airport time, the flight had arrived on schedule.

A similar experience providing us with more detail concerns another private pilot, Bruce Gernon. In December 1970 Gernon was flying from Andros Island to Palm Beach when, at a height of around 3,000 feet, he flew into an enormous elliptical cloud. Inside the cloud the aircraft's instrument panel showed all instruments malfunctioning. Espying a hole in the cloud, Gernon sped towards it. In so doing he seemed to be travelling through a tunnel of sorts and, for a few seconds, experienced a total loss of gravity. As he emerged into the open Gernon saw an island beneath him and then, just as suddenly, Miami airfield came into view. After landing at Palm Beach the astonished Gernon discovered that he had completed the trip half an hour ahead of schedule and that the aircraft had consumed only a fraction of the amount of fuel he should have needed for the 200-mile trip. Had Gernon flown into another dimension in which time ran very quickly?

Further 'corroboration' for this theory comes from the Bermuda Triangle researcher Richard Winer, who organized a flight through the area for a number of clairvoyants. One of these psychics, in a state of hypnotic trance, claimed to take on the identity of a pilot by the name of Gallivan. Gallivan had been a member of Flight 19, a gunner who had flown with Captain Stivers. 'Gallivan', through the clairvoyant, referred to an approaching storm with an unusual cloud pattern. There followed references to lack of visibility and malfunctioning instruments:

> I can't tell the water from the air. I have no control. Ahead there is an opening . . . a clearing . . . something like a crack of light under a door. It seems like an escape from the storm. The plane is flying toward it, but I have no control. It's sort of like a vacuum. . . . Ahead is a long cylindrical object. The end is open and parts of planes are being pulled inside. . . .

References to UFOs and obscure energy sources followed these disclosures, but the details provided above seem to bear an uncanny resemblance to Bruce Gernon's experiences. Having made this observation it must still be said that perhaps we are, after all, making too much of a mystery out of Flight 19's disappearance.

Only 12 months earlier, in December 1944, a flight of seven US Air Force bombers came to grief off Bermuda. Without warning, all the aircraft were suddenly flung downwards towards the ocean. Only two crews managed to gain control over their planes. The rest crashed into the sea and were lost without trace, victims of the curious phenomenon of clear air turbulence. Had it not been for the two surviving crews the flight could well have appropriated the place of Flight 19 in the annals of modern folklore.

But Flight 19's loss was no sudden catastrophe. The agony of the Air Force bombers in 1944 was over in seconds. Flight 19 took four hours to die, and it is this circumstance, together with the fact that the flight was continuously in radio contact with would-be rescuers, that raises the mystery out of the ordinary and into the extraordinary.

As the years roll by, what little new evidence comes to light tends, if anything, to deepen the mystery. Three facts suggest that Flight 19 was indeed over the Florida Keys. Firstly, Taylor himself believed that such was his position. For the previous six months he had been based at the Miami naval air station. He must have flown over the Keys on many occasions, and it is difficult to see how he could easily have been mistaken. Secondly, Port Everglades, situated to the south of Fort Lauderdale, maintained radio contact with Flight 19 long after the latter station had lost it. Finally, the Avenger wreckage dredged up off Key West in 1987 suggests that the flight may have ditched in that area.

If this were true, then nonsense would be made of the radio-fix, obtained from information supplied by six different stations, which put Flight 19 to the north of the Bahamas. How, then, can this conflicting evidence be reconciled?

Critics of the Bermuda Triangle hypothesis usually fall back, rather lamely, on the last resort of anyone gamely searching for a logical answer to mysterious disappearances in the air:

human error. Certainly human error, combined with the fatigue syndrome, contributed in the past to many passenger airline disasters. Errors of judgement have even been known to afflict both captain and co-pilot simultaneously on the always critical subject of flight altitude. Flight 19, however, with a personnel of 14, should have been able to muster sufficient expertise to override any inkling of human error which may have been present. The veterans among their number had been accustomed to flying sorties from the decks of aircraft carriers in the mid-Pacific and to finding their way back afterwards – to the landing deck of what was literally a speck in the ocean which would itself have shifted position in the time between take-off and landing. Is it reasonable to suppose that these very same men were now unable to find the east coast of the United States after a routine afternoon flight?

The subsequent Board of Investigation seemed to think not, issuing a statement to the effect that there was no explanation which could be offered for what had occurred. The loss, the board concluded, would go down as one of the great mysteries of naval aviation. And so it has.

8

PROJECT
INVISIBILITY

The military mind has always been intrigued by the concept of camouflage and the possibilities it offers for outwitting one's enemies. Until comparatively recently the essence of camouflage lay in the practice of covering men and machines with leafage within the confines of a wooded area. The degree of sophistication has advanced over the years although the principle has remained the same.

During the Second World War a new dimension was added to the subject with the introduction of radar – the use of high-powered radio pulses directed at, and reflected from, objects for the purpose of identification of location and subsequent destruction. Today the threat posed by radar has been defeated by advances in design technology. The deflected radio pulses which constitute the radar principle can be minimized – indeed, eliminated altogether – by the avoidance of ninety-degree angles in the design of a ship or an aircraft, within which radar pulses are most effectively deflected back to the detector source. Only the literal 'disappearance' of an object could represent an improvement on such a line of defence. In the summer of 1943 it has been claimed that just such an event occurred: the actual disappearance – engineered by the US Navy – of a destroyer, the USS *Eldridge*.

The story first came to public attention through a shadowy, ephemeral figure called Carlos Allende, an ordinary seaman who claimed to have witnessed the event in its entirety. Allende lived with his story for 12 years before finally telling it to Dr Morris Jessup, scientist and author of *The Case for the UFO*. Allende chose Jessup as his confidant because the crux of Jessup's argument in support of UFO phenomena concerned the harnessing of the earth's gravitational field as a source of energy for powering spacecraft.

Towards the end of 1955 Jessup received a letter from Allende in which it was implied that Einstein's unified field theory had been brought to fruition by the United States Navy, the result being the complete invisibility of the *Eldridge* and all its crew. According to Allende, 'The Field was effective in an oblate, spheroidal shape, extending 100 yards. Any person within that sphere became vague in form, while any person without that sphere could see nothing save the clearly defined shape of the ship's hull in the water.' Allende further alleged that the *Eldridge* later 'disappeared' from its Philadelphia dock, appearing only moments later at Newport News, Norfolk, before 'returning' to its former location.

On the issue of Einstein's unified field theory one is partly hamstrung by the authorities' understandable obsession with secrecy, for it is unclear to the general enquirer just how far Einstein progressed with work on this theory. Basically the unified field concept involves an attempt to find a theory which reduces the natural forces – gravity, electromagnetic and nuclear – to a single unified force. An electric field created in a coil induces a magnetic field at right angles to it, each of the fields representing one spatial plane. However, as there are three spatial planes it follows that there should also be a gravitational one, which it should be possible to produce through the principle of resonance with the use of eletromagnetic generators. The creation of what was in effect a tremendous magnetic field around the vessel to which Allende referred, caused it to enter a time-space warp – thus rendering it invisible to percipients at the time of the experiment.

Einstein had developed his unified field theory in the early 1920s. Realizing its imperfections he subjected it to continuous modification. But with the facilities placed at his disposal during the 1930s following his emigration from Germany to the United States and, in particular, with the encouragement and co-operation of the US Navy, for which he worked in the war years, it is possible that by 1943 an advanced version of the unified field theory was ready to be applied in practice.

Morris Jessup's own interest in the unified field theory lay in its possibilities for explaining the motive power behind UFOs. Critics of the UFO hypothesis have argued against their existence in terms of the vast distances which spacecraft would have to travel in order to reach the Earth. This thinking is based upon the limitations of known rocket power. But suppose the natural forces could be harnessed – as in the unified field theory – so as to permit the breakdown of a molecular structure with its subsequent reassembly at another place and, indeed, at another time? Given that such an experiment was theoretically possible, how convincing are Allende's allegations?

Allende claimed that he was a crew member of an observer vessel, the USS *Andrew Furuseth*, which monitored the Philadelphia Experiment, as it came to be known. According to Allende the trials were never intended to render the subject matter (ie the *Eldridge*) 'invisible' within the strictest definition of the term. The vessel in question was, rather, shielded from the observers behind a force field which he described as a greenish sort of 'transparent fog'. By way of preliminary findings the results, according to Allende, were encouraging, although subsequent developmental work was accorded a relatively low priority. Towards the end of 1943 it was apparent that the Allies were winning the war by conventional means, and such 'unconventional' research as did take place was directed wholeheartedly towards the development of the atomic bomb.

As devastating as the visible results of the trials must have been, these were overshadowed in Allende's mind by something more sinister – the unexpected effect of the unified field upon the *Eldridge* crew members. Although Allende was prepared to allow that the experiment was a complete success, the men involved, he proclaimed chillingly, were 'complete failures'. Half the officers and crew went mad. In 1955 a few of them were still under restraint in security establishments where, from time to time, they suffered bouts of 'invisibility' – a condition Allende referred to as 'freezing' and which the victims themselves called 'Hell Incorporated'. Release from this condition depended upon the 'laying on of hands' by those who were unaffected. Of the handful who were left alive, one, in full view of his wife and children, had walked through a wall and was never seen again.

By way of support for this fantastic catalogue of events, Allende quoted a newspaper article about the crew's visit to a dockside bar immediately after the experiment where they 'caused such shock and paralysis of the waitresses that little comprehensible could be gotten from them'. He even named some crew members who could substantiate his story: Chief Mate Mowsley and Richard Price.

But Jessup was not Allende's only correspondent. Allende had also sent a personally annotated copy of Jessup's *The Case for the UFO* to Washington DC. Allende's scribblings concerning the Philadelphia Experiment, taken in conjunction with Jessup's text, interested the authorities to such an extent that they invited Jessup to Washington in the spring of 1957. They even insisted on examining the Allende–Jessup correspondence, and went to the length of producing copies of the annotated text.

Jessup lived alone – his children had grown up and he was separated from his wife – and travelled a good deal, so it is difficult to evaluate his state of mind. But it is clear that by the autumn of 1958 he feared for his safety. He had in his possession one of the Washington-produced annotated copies of *The Case for the UFO*, in which he made further notes of his own. On a visit to his friend Ivan T. Sanderson (a writer and authority on the Bermuda Triangle), Jessup handed him this particular edition, begging him to place it under lock and key in case 'anything should happen to me'.

Shortly after this incident Jessup was involved in a car accident, from which he took a considerable time to recuperate. Jessup's own story ended on 20 April 1959, when he was discovered in Dade County Park, Florida, his car full of carbon monoxide fumes introduced by means of a hose attached to the exhaust pipe. The verdict was one of suicide, although it was not explained why Jessup should choose to drive several miles to carry out a form of suicide which could have been executed more efficiently and conveniently in his own garage.

It seems that Jessup had been on his way to keep a dinner engagement with another friend, Dr J. Manson Valentine (who, like Sanderson, had a keen interest in the Bermuda Triangle). Jessup had prepared the rough draft of a paper concerning some important conclusions he had reached about the Philadelphia Experiment. It is perhaps suggestive that no documents were found in Jessup's car on that April night in 1959. Valentine himself always reminded friends and colleagues that Jessup,

91

when found, had still been alive, and posed the question whether sufficient effort had been made to save him.

Yet the key to assessing the validity of the Philadelphia Experiment must surely lie in an assessment of the credibility of the man who first drew public attention to it: Carlos Allende himself.

What sort of person was he? The truth is that very little is known about him. Even though he has submitted to interviews he has displayed a knack of parting with very little information about himself. One of the most fruitful interviews was conducted by the author William Moore, who persuaded Allende to name the ship used in the experiment. He identified it as the USS *Eldridge*. As for Allende personally, virtually all that is known about him is that he has spent a lifetime drifting from job to job, with the exception of his years at sea dating from 1943 to 1952.

Allende's lack of academic credentials need not cast doubt on his claims. He was asked for 'the facts' and he provided them by naming the *Eldridge* as the experimental ship, the *Andrew Furuseth* as the vessel which witnessed the experiment, and by identifying crew members other than himself who could, if they chose to do so, substantiate his story. Had Allende intended a hoax it is unlikely he would have produced corroborative evidence in terms of names which could be checked.

It is not Allende's fault that efforts to track down both the crew members he named and records relating to the *Andrew Furuseth* reached a dead end. Chief Mate Mowlsey was traced, but investigators met with a wall of silence when the Philadelphia Experiment was mentioned. Richard Price, William Moore discovered, died in 1973. With the passage of nearly half a century since the Philadelphia Experiment took place, there is little hope that either eyewitnesses or primary source material will now be traced.

As far as documentary evidence is concerned, matters have reached a similar impasse. The log of the *Eldridge* for the latter half of 1943 is classed as 'missing' while all the logs of the *Andrew Furuseth* have been destroyed. The problem, then, is to demonstrate that both vessels were in the same place at the same time as claimed by Allende.

It is reasonable to suppose that a top secret operation such as the Philadelphia Experiment undoubtedly was, would hardly be recorded in detail in the log of either ship, although the logs would certainly have stated the location of both – hence their unavailability. Given that this information may have been eradicated (for obvious reasons) could it not also be the case that such records as do exist could, at the very least, have been subjected to amendment?

In their immaculately researched book on the Philadelphia Experiment, Charles Berlitz and William Moore suggested that the *Eldridge* was launched a month earlier than the records show – ie, on 25 June 1943 as opposed to the official launching date of 25 July 1943 – and that she lay in dock in the Philadelphia area, from where she put to sea in late July or early August for trials in the Bermuda area.

As for the *Andrew Furuseth* it has been possible to trace her movements from records other than the official log. From these sources it has been substantiated that on 13 August 1943 she left New York on a voyage to North Africa, during the preliminary stages of which she sailed down the coastline to Norfolk, leaving there on 16 August. During the course of both her manoeuvres and those of the *Eldridge* it becomes a distinct possibility that their paths could have crossed – with an opportunity for the crew of the *Furuseth* to witness any experiment along the lines of that which Allende claimed had taken place.

As critics have eagerly pointed out, Allende stated that the incident occurred in the autumn of 1943 – in late September or early October. But 13 years had elapsed between the event and Allende's communications with Jessup, and it seems reasonable to ascribe the discrepancy of a matter of weeks to a lapse of memory. If asked to pinpoint dates of significance in our own lives we would be hard pressed to do so with any degree of competence had we to go back a dozen years or more.

An odd sidelight on the affair concerns a certain Dr Franklin Reno, yet another name cited by Allende in his voluminous correspondence with Jessup. According to Allende, Dr Reno (with whom he claimed to be on friendly terms) had provided some of the mathematical computations which had made the Philadelphia Experiment possible. During the course of their research Berlitz and Moore discovered that 'Reno' was merely a pseudonym. Thus Moore's success in tracking him down is doubly commendable.

Reno stressed that his continued anonymity was essential to his well-being, as was the reclusive lifestyle he led. He went on to confirm his involvement in the project – on the lines suggested by Allende. He also drew attention to the dichotomy between theory and practice which led to the imperfect results, explaining that the ionization created by the unified field caused an uneven refraction of the light, leading to the creation of what he described aptly as a 'confused area', as opposed to a disappearance *per se*. Although Reno had warned of the possible dangers involved, the US Navy clearly went ahead without troubling itself to address the issue.

A further point of interest is the newspaper report concerning the mayhem caused by the visit by *Eldridge* crew members to a dockside bar. Again, the reference provided by Allende was precise: '. . . a tiny one Paragraph (upper Half of sheet, inside the paper Near the rear 3rd of Paper, 1944–46 in Spring or Fall or Winter, NOT Summer. . . .' This is the sort of reference which rings true. You remember a newspaper article which made an impression on you at the time you read it. You remember the portion of the newspaper and also where the article appeared on the page. But the nature of your work means that you are continuously on the move, and you cannot recall the name of the newspaper or the exact date of the particular issue. You wished you had cut out the article and kept it, but you did not.

The article itself has defied all attempts made to trace it. However, a photocopy of it has surfaced, and describes the bar brawl as depicted by Allende. It bears no reference which enables it to be tied down to any particular publication – but how many news clippings do? In the article, the reporter makes reference to the arrival of the military police immediately after 'two of the sailors involved allegedly did a disappearing act. "They just sort of vanished into thin air . . . right there," reported one of the frightened hostesses.' The article concludes with a comment from one of the more cynical bystanders: '. . . a lot of hooey from them daffy dames down there.'

Another issue often lost in the welter of claims and counter-claims surrounding the practicalities of the Philadelphia Experiment proper is Allende's subsidiary assertion that the *Eldridge* had disappeared from its Philadelphia dock to another in the Norfolk area before reappearing again in Philadelphia. Little or no evidence has been found to support this claim. Allende did not witness the alleged event himself, and by way of support he could produce only a vague reference to another newspaper article. Although the suggestion cannot be written off – particularly if it is accepted that the major incident involving the *Eldridge* and the *Furuseth* took place – it may well be that Allende's memory is at fault here. Could he be mixing up this newspaper article with the one about the dockside bar room brawl? On balance it seems that this 'follow-up' incident is something of a red herring, and it should not be allowed to detract from the main story.

Allende's memory displays only the failings of our own memories, yet much has been done to attack his degree of reliability as a witness. In this connection there is one potential extenuating circumstance not mentioned by other investigators: could Allende himself have suffered physical harm from his proximity to the unified force field, in much the same way that distant witnesses of a nuclear explosion might suffer from the effects of fall-out? The entire crew of the *Furuseth* could have been so affected. And what of the genetic effects of such damage in the offspring of crew members of both the *Furuseth* and *Eldridge*? That the Philadelphia Experiment was imperfect in its results is not surprising. Unified field theory research has made but slow progress in the past 50 years, making the deficiencies of the theory as it stood in 1943 only too apparent.

A feature film entitled *The Philadelphia Experiment*, brought to the big screen in 1984, tended only to complicate matters. In the movie the experiment took place in October 1943 which, as we have seen, was unlikely. It was also presented as occurring in a barely offshore location in a densely populated area – again rather unlikely. The script concentrated on the adventures of two *Eldridge* crew members who were projected into the future through a hole in the space-time continuum, to find the scientist responsible – a fictional Dr James Longstreet – indulging in another, equally disastrous present-day experiment.

To embroider the story of 'Project Invisibility' proves unnecessary. The facts as they stand provide more than sufficient substance for the ultimate chilling horror story of our time.

9

INTO THIN AIR

Amelia Earhart

Female flyers have always possessed a certain kind of kudos, commanding that special mixture of admiration and prestige reserved for women who succeed in a traditionally male-dominated profession. During the 1930s, in what were pioneering days for long-distance flying, each country had its very own heroine of the air: Hanna Reitsch, German test pilot and glider champion; Madeleine Charnaux, the captivating Frenchwoman who flew to a record height of 20,000 feet in a light aircraft; plucky Amy Johnson, whose solo flights to Australia and the Cape of Good Hope gained her enormous popularity with the British public. The United States, meanwhile, was represented by a slim, delicate girl sporting an air of bright, boyish innocence – Amelia Earhart.

Born in Kansas in 1898 of professional parents, Amelia grew up wanting to be a nurse, a profession she subsequently found satisfying enough. But in 1921, after her first flight as a passenger in an old biplane, she was determined to become a pilot herself. It was an ambition she accomplished with the aid of her mother, who bought her first plane.

Her big chance came in 1928, when she was asked to take part in a flight across the Atlantic, although only as a passenger. The flight went smoothly enough, and even though, in her own words, Amelia had been just 'a piece of luggage', she had become the first woman to cross the Atlantic by air. A by-product of the undertaking was her marriage to the publisher George Putnam, who had been heavily involved in publicizing the flight. The union was never consummated, both parties appearing to favour

96

Five Avenger torpedo bombers of the type which disappeared off the Florida coast in December 1945, the first incident in the so-called 'Bermuda Triangle'.

left: Amelia Earhart and her husband George Putnam preparing for her ill-fated round the world flight in 1937. The kites were to be released as a signal in the case of a forced landing. *below:* Amelia Earhart with the single engined Lockheed Vega in which she made her record-breaking solo Atlantic flight to Ireland in 1932.

my Johnson, Britain's celebrated aviatrix, in the cabin of her plane 'Desert Cloud'. Her flying
reer had taken her all over the world, but it was while she was on a routine flight over Britain
uring the Second World War that she mysteriously vanished.

The Tudor IVB, 'Star Ariel', which became the third aeroplane operated by BSAAC to disappear within two years when it vanished on a flight from Nassau to Kingston, Jamaica in January 1949. This disappearance was particularly baffling as the last communication from 'Star Ariel' indicated that she was flying at a good height, in clear skies, and with ample fuel.

an arrangement whereby each respected the other's personal freedom and dignity.

Amelia's finest hour came in 1932 when, with the magnanimous Putnam's backing, she made her very own solo Atlantic flight, from Newfoundland to Limerick, bettering Charles Lindbergh's time by three hours. She became the toast of America and Europe, with life one hectic round of receptions, lunches and evening-dress banquets. But even the most delirious success has its own drawbacks. The problem was that, at 34 years of age, Amelia had reached the peak of her profession. What was there left for her to do? She continued to fly all over the world – Mexico, Brazil, India – largely for pleasure, while secretly harbouring a desire for more conquests to rival the achievement of the solo Atlantic crossing.

Ultimately, in 1937, she found the project she had been looking for in a 27,000-mile flight around the world by the longest route, the Equator – another potential 'first'. After a false start early in the year involving a crash-landing in Honolulu, Amelia took off from Oakland, California, on 1 June in a twin-engined 600-horsepower Lockheed Electra. On this occasion she was accompanied by a navigator, Fred Noonan, who has been described as thoroughly reliable and with a perfect mastery of his job. In fact he was an alcoholic for whom the trip was an adjunct to the 'drying-out' process he had recently undergone.

The venture appeared to be an outstanding success. From Oakland the route took Amelia and Noonan to Miami via Lafayette, to Brazil and then on to Dakar, Khartoum, Rangoon, Singapore, Darwin and New Guinea, where the pair landed at Lae on 30 June. At 10am on 2 July they set off on the final lap, from Lae to Howland Island and thence to Honolulu and Oakland.

It may have been the last lap but it was certainly the most difficult. The stretch of ocean between Lae and Howland Island had never before been flown. Very little shipping used the route so that there would be little chance of rescue if they ran into trouble. And trouble there might be, for there was a head-wind and storm clouds were gathering. More seriously, Noonan was having problems with the chronometers, which seemed to have developed a fault. Clearly, Amelia should never have taken off. Perhaps she thought her luck would hold.

Vanished!

A United States Coast Guard cutter, *Itasca*, waited patiently off Howland Island for the Electra's approach; a second, *Ontario*, was stationed at the flight's mid-point. The plan was for Amelia to make routine transmissions at half-hourly intervals. Although the *Ontario* was unable to make any radio contact at all with her, it was not thought that the *Itasca*, supported by sensitive direction-finding equipment on Howland, would experience any difficulties in this respect. In fact the *Itasca* made her own regular transmissions to help the Electra pinpoint the tiny speck of land, barely half a mile wide, nestling in the vast expanse of the Pacific Ocean.

But Amelia's broadcasts were intermittent and laden with static, and made reference to windy conditions and cloud cover. After 5am on 3 July, when the Electra had been in the air for 19 hours, it became apparent that Amelia and Noonan were in trouble. Although Amelia was making increasingly desperate calls for a bearing, she was not staying on the air long enough for the Howland Coast Guard to obtain a fix.

The Electra's estimated time of arrival, 6.30am, came and went. The last message of all came in at 8.45am with Amelia, panic-stricken, pleading for assistance, but by this time the batteries running the direction finder on Howland were flat. At 10.30am the *Itasca* embarked on a search in the area immediately around the island in the forlorn hope of spotting the aircraft which must surely, by now, have ditched into the sea. The full, futile search, involving the US Pacific Fleet, went on for two weeks and cost a staggering $4 million.

The search had two particularly tragic aspects. One was the series of SOS calls allegedly overheard by ham radio operators, suggesting that the Electra was still afloat somewhere north of Howland. These reports were later embroidered by romantics who claimed that the signals were at first clear, indicating that they had been transmitted by the experienced navigator, Noonan. Later signals received were confused, implying that they were sent by Amelia after Noonan had courageously leapt into the shark-infested waters to enable the Electra to remain afloat.

The second unfortunate aspect concerned another female pioneer of the air, Jacqueline Cochrane, who claimed to possess psychic powers. Amelia and a badly injured Noonan, she said, were alive, afloat on the ditched aircraft.

The search to the north stretched as far as the Marshall Islands, 500 miles distant from Howland and then under Japanese control. A rumour took hold to the effect that Amelia had been on a spying mission aimed at taking aerial photographs of Japanese military installations in the Marshalls and that she had been taken prisoner by the Japanese. Some fuel was added to this unlikely hypothesis in 1944 when Marshall Islanders told the invading American Marines of two American flyers, a man and a woman, who had been taken by the Japanese seven years before. The woman had died of dysentery, the man beheaded by his captors. A photograph of Amelia was even found on the body of a dead Japanese soldier on Okinawa.

Amelia had worked closely with the US government in the planning of her final undertaking, but this was purely because the direction-finding equipment on Howland was a top-secret development. Its application to the Electra flight was experimental in nature and a highly sensitive issue. Yet the Japanese theory has its adherents even today. In 1989 the International Group for Historic Aviation Recovery announced that an expedition to Nikumaroro, 500 miles to the south of Howland Island, had unearthed several artefacts including a cigarette lighter and a pre-war aircraft battery. This led to the proposal of a scenario in which the Electra crash-landed there, with Earhart and Noonan surviving for days before dying of thirst. Investigations continue along this line of enquiry.

The real solution to the disappearance of Amelia Earhart is probably much simpler. That Noonan was unable to locate Howland – the proverbial speck in the ocean – is no reflection upon his ability as a navigator. Take-off from Lae should have been delayed until better weather conditions prevailed. As it was, poor visibility made an already difficult task all that much harder, while strong head-winds made for a considerable handicap in terms of increased fuel consumption, with less to spare for any emergency. The Electra carried no emergency portable radio and no flares. A combination of poor organization and impatience led to the doom of America's foremost aviatrix.

Glenn Miller

When a celebrity disappears in mysterious circumstances the authorities find it difficult to discourage public curiosity. On occasions the official explanation, hastily improvised and unconvincing, encourages suspicion on its own account. Such an example concerns the mysterious disappearance of the world-famous bandleader Glenn Miller, who vanished on 15 December 1944.

Glenn Miller was born in 1904 in the mid-western state of Iowa. His childhood was spent in comparatively poor circumstances, although his family background was a musical one and, by dint of hard work, he managed to acquire a trombone. In due course he dropped out of university to take up the uncertain life of a professional musician and arranger. His employers included Ben Pollack, Red Nichols, the Dorsey Brothers and Ray Noble. But he was still struggling to find his own distinctive sound. He succeeded almost by accident when, in the mid-1930s, during a second attempt to form his own band, the absence of a trumpet player compelled him to arrange for a combination of clarinet and saxophones to replace the traditional dominant trumpet lead.

It was a classic example of 'overnight success' following years of hard work and application. Classic compositions such as 'Moonlight Serenade', 'String of Pearls' and 'In the Mood' made Miller both a household name and a millionaire. And then, at the height of his fame, the United States entered the Second World War. Along with other famous stars like James Stewart and Clark Gable, Miller joined the USAAF, and formed his famous American Air Force Band with the intention of entertaining the troops. Following the Normandy landings in June 1944, this meant travelling to Britain to broadcast to the invasion forces.

The band was based away from the Blitz in Bedford, from where regular BBC broadcasts were made. Connoisseurs consider Miller's band at this time to be his best, comprising the cream of conscripted popular and classical musicians. But Miller wanted to take his music to the troops in person, planning to follow in the wake of the forces. In particular he developed a scheme for the organization of a Christmas concert in Paris, which had fallen to the allies in August 1944. He contrived to fulfil his obligations to the BBC by recording six weeks' radio broadcasts in advance. The BBC was satisfied and the Paris concert duly set up.

The band was due to be flown out to Paris in three USAAF transport aircraft but bad weather delayed departure. Worried about final arrangements for the concert, Miller decided to go on ahead and succeeded in getting a lift in a light aircraft, a 600-horsepower Norseman, on a non-operational flight to Bordeaux. On the morning of 15 December 1944 the Norseman, piloted by Flying Officer John Morgan, took off from Abbots Ripton in Huntingdonshire and made for the RAF airfield at Twinwood Farm near Bedford to pick up Miller and his friend, Lt-Colonel Norman Baessell, who had arranged Miller's flight for him. The Norseman, with Miller and Baessel on board, departed from Twinwood on the second leg of its journey at 1.55pm. It was never heard from again.

The band followed on 18 December. On arrival in Paris its members expected to find Miller there to meet them, but learned only that he had not arrived as scheduled and that no one knew where he was. An air, if not of secrecy, then certainly of reticence clouded the efforts of Miller's manager, Don Haynes, to clarify the issue. The BBC continued to broadcast the pre-recorded concerts and it was not until 23 December that the USAAF felt obliged to post Miller as 'missing'.

By its own silence the USAAF encouraged many ill-founded rumours about Glenn Miller's fate. As with all rumours an element of truth, however small, must exist to provide them with a flimsy basis. For example, it was claimed that Miller had been involved in black-market activities and that, discovered, he had been forced to abscond. This arose because Miller's fellow passenger, Norman Baessell, carried on a small trade in black-market items on his frequent trips to France, as indeed did many of the officers who flew regularly between Britain and the Continent. According to another rumour Miller had reached Paris and been found dead in a red-light district. Despite James Stewart's portrayal of Miller as a doting husband in *The Glenn Miller Story*, the man himself was an inveterate womanizer and his discovery in a red-light district might not be totally incongruous.

Other rumours came rather closer to the probable reality, involving the Norseman crash-landing. One such theory proposes a crash-landing in fog in a heavily wooded area where the plane still lies, half-buried, awaiting discovery. A variation on this story has Miller surviving such a crash but being so hideously disfigured that he chose to live out the remainder of his life in seclusion. Other Miller fans claim that he had never gone to France at all but had died of tuberculosis in a military hospital. Photographs of Miller taken between 1942 and 1944 do suggest a progressive decline in physical condition, although this is likely to have occurred through the punishing work schedule he set both for his orchestra and himself.

As far as the weather is concerned, although most air traffic was fog-bound at the time of Miller's flight, conditions over the Channel were much clearer with a forecast of 'intermittent rains, stratus clouds, ceiling 1,000–2,000 feet, southerly wind of 2 miles per hour, warm front'. And even if the Norseman had been forced to ditch into the Channel, the chances of being picked up were high. Neither is it likely that the aircraft was shot down by a German fighter. The Luftwaffe was no longer able to offer air protection to its own ground forces and it is extremely unlikely that fighters would be spared to patrol the Channel on the off-chance of bagging the occasional scrap of allied traffic.

Another possibility sometimes put forward is that the Norseman iced-up and ditched in the Channel. However, there was no rain on that day, effectively precluding the major cause of icing. Carburretor icing, which is not dependent upon rainfall but on humidity, would also have been unlikely as the aircraft was fitted with a heating device. In any event such an emergency would have allowed time for the transmission of a Mayday signal, yet none was received.

This leaves just one possibility: that Miller's aircraft was brought down by allied activity. In his efforts to evade the fog it is possible that Flying Officer Morgan flew into restricted airspace. It may be that this is what happened, the Norseman being brought down by a Spitfire. A viable alternative is suggested by the recollections of a Lancaster bomber crew returning to base following an aborted raid. They were jettisoning their load into the Channel within a specified area to the south of Beachy Head. While dropping several tons of bombs into the sea from a height of 4,500 feet, three crew members saw a light aircraft, which they identified as a Norseman, fly into the restricted area and dive into the ocean after being hit by their incendiaries. Curiously enough they did not make any reference to the incident until 40 years later, when the navigator recounted the story at an ex-servicemen's reunion.

From time to time fresh intelligence comes to light. In 1985, for example, a salvage businessman, Clive Ward, claimed to have found the Norseman on the sea bed lying 80 feet down, a few miles west of Le Touquet. Ward himself ascribes to the theory that Miller was found in the Parisienne red-light district. The Norseman located by Ward is empty and he believes that it was deliberately ditched to cover up the scandalous truth.

Another perspective on the problem has been provided by the clairvoyant Carmen Rogers, who has visited the derelict Twinwood site and has 'tuned in' to the past. She suggests that Miller, worried about personal and business affairs, did not wish to go to Paris, and in mid-flight asked Morgan to put down before they reached the Channel, enabling Miller to make arrangements for his own disappearance. However, Miller was at the height of his success, he was planning to build a dream-house for his family and the Paris trip was, if anything, an obsessive preoccupation.

One final intriguing rumour concerns the suspicion that, at the time of his disappearance, Miller was carrying original scores of music never before played – which should provide a spur for any salvage experts. Hopefully the manuscripts were carried in a watertight container. No one can deny the personal tragedy in Miller's comparatively early death. From a professional viewpoint, however, Miller's demise – if he did die – occurred at exactly the right time, providing him with the aura of mystery and charisma of the shining star snuffed out when at its brightest.

Amy Johnson

During the Second World War it was almost a routine matter for aircraft to be posted 'missing', but when the pilot was someone as famous as Amy Johnson the incident was lifted out of the ordinary to become a matter of grave public concern.

Amy Johnson was born in Hull in 1903, the daughter of a successful fish merchant. A lonely childhood, during which she displayed more interest in boys' games than in traditional girls' pastimes, was followed by three years at Sheffield University, where she graduated with an honours degree in economics in 1925. Despite this achievement she drifted aimlessly from one dead-end office job to another, her fitfulness being heightened by a long and unhappy love-affair. Popular legend has it that when her lover took up with another woman, Amy turned to flying 'on the rebound', in much the same way as other girls might have rushed headlong into an alternative, dangerous liaison.

Nevertheless, despite a shaky start (including an assurance from her flying instructor that she had no hope of gaining her licence), she succeeded both in qualifying as a pilot and in becoming only the second woman to qualify as a ground engineer. Upon gaining the engineer's qualification in December 1929 she immediately began planning for a solo flight to make her name. Almost anything would do, provided it counted as a 'first'. She chose Australia, which had already been 'done' by an Australian pilot, Bert Hinkler, who had taken 15 days to complete the trip from Britain in 1928. Her aim was to beat his record. Should she fail, she would still achieve the distinction of being the first woman to finish the mission.

The stumbling block was lack of money. Newspapers and industrialists remained largely deaf to her pleas. Ultimately, Lord Wakefield, the oil magnate, together with her father, supplied the necessary funds that enabled Amy to buy a second-hand Gipsy Moth.

On 5 May 1930, with little media attention, she took off from Croydon airport – just 10 months after qualifying as a pilot and with only 75 hours' flying time behind her. The route she planned took her to Vienna, Aleppo, Baghdad and Karachi, at which point she found herself two days ahead of Hinkler's time. She had also suddenly become headline news. The remainder of the flight went less smoothly, with atrocious weather conditions and poorly executed landings (for which she was famous throughout her life) so that Hinkler's record slipped from her grasp. She landed in Darwin after nineteen and a half days. But it was enough to make her into a star – and a star she remained.

Her personal life now came under the spotlight, in particular her marriage in 1932 to another well-known flyer, Jim Mollison. They became the 'Flying Sweethearts' even though, professionally, they remained rivals and personally were unsuited as a result of Mollison's heavy drinking and womanizing. Mollison held the record of four and a half days for the England to Cape Town run, but by the end of 1932 Amy herself had taken the record, outstripping her husband's time by 10 hours. In an effort to stem his rising resentment at her continuing success, Amy suggested a joint venture in which they would make an attempt on the world long-distance flight record on a Britain – New York – Baghdad – London circuit. At the second attempt (the first ended in a crash on take-off), Mollison crash-landed their twin-engined de Havilland at Bridgeport, Connecticut, after having irresponsibly run short of fuel.

A further joint venture, also doomed to failure, was their entry in the 1934 England to Australia air race. Although they reached Karachi in only 22 hours, they foundered on the second leg. When flying with Mollison, Amy always seemed to founder. In 1936, again flying solo, she set up a new record on the London – Cape Town route.

By the outbreak of the Second World War, Amy had all but retired from competition. Her marriage to Mollison had ended inevitably in divorce, and she had been shocked by the death of Amelia Earhart two years before. Ten years of the high-life had made a dent in the wealth she had acquired from her success. She was now earning a modest living as a ferry pilot on the south coast, when the company for which she worked was taken over by the RAF. Amy had little choice but to apply for a job with the Air Transport Auxiliary, where she found herself on equal terms with the inexperienced young socialites who comprised the membership. Not unreasonably she felt that her skills and experience were not being employed to the full.

Amy's work involved delivering aircraft to various fields throughout the country. On 4 January 1941 she was instructed to

105

ferry a twin-engined Oxford from Prestwick to Kidlington. She flew down from Prestwick to Squires Gate in Lancashire, staying overnight with her sister in Blackpool. She took off from Squires Gate in the late morning of 5 January – against advice, which reported a proliferation of low cloud in the Midlands. But Amy was nothing if not persistent.

At about 3.30pm on 5 January a coastal convoy was passing through the Thames Estuary. A number of seamen heard the drone of an aircraft which soon came into view, circling overhead. At least one and possibly two parachutists were seen to plummet into the sea, followed by the gently spiralling aircraft.

One of the convoy escort vessels, HMS *Haslemere*, tried to give assistance. It appeared that there were two survivors in the water and that one was a woman who, apparently unable to grasp ropes thrown to her, disappeared under the stern. The *Haslemere*'s captain, Lt-Commander Fletcher, swam out to the other survivor. Having reached his goal he then turned back. Fletcher himself, following 10 minutes in the icy waters, lost consciousness and died later in the day from hypothermia. A subsequent scan of the area led to the discovery of two bags floating in the water. One contained Amy Johnson's log-book.

This would seem to confirm that one of the parachutists was Amy. But who was the mysterious second person? And who was the third person who appeared to be flying the aeroplane while Amy and her companion ditched into the sea? Why was Amy flying over the Thames Estuary at 3.30pm when she should have landed at Kidlington, 100 miles away, some two and a half hours earlier?

One of the more sinister theories proposed at the time was that Amy had flown over to France on a secret mission, perhaps to collect a secret agent. Another, prevalent among friends, was that she was so depressed over the break-up of her marriage that she had deliberately flown out to sea as a means of committing suicide.

A much more likely scenario to fit the facts would run as follows: Amy's Oxford carried neither radio nor navigation aid. In overcast conditions she was flying 'blind'. It is not inconceivable that she veered much further eastwards than she had intended. The convoy escort ships carried barrage balloons which they were flying at about 2,000 feet. By 3.30pm the

Oxford was running out of fuel and Amy, sighting the barrage balloons, presumed that she was over land and thought it would be safe to bale out. To do this she used the rear exit door, which had to be jettisoned in order to make a jump. The seamen thought they saw two people hitting the water when, in fact, they saw only Amy. The other shape was the door. Bobbing up and down in choppy seas and possibly tangled up with the bags later recovered, it could easily have been mistaken for a second person. Fletcher turned back when he had swum far enough out to realize this. There was no third person flying the Oxford which spiralled gently down, borne up by air currents, before plummeting into the Channel.

Even though the incident occurred in 1941 it was not until 1943 that Amy Johnson was officially declared dead, her place in the history and development of British aviation assured.

Leslie Howard

Leslie Howard was one of the best loved British film stars of the inter-war years. He was also one of the most admired and respected, an essentially classical actor who had succeeded in Hollywood. An enigmatic individual, he was as endearing in real life as many of the characters he played on screen.

Howard, who claimed Hungarian descent, was born in London in 1893. Educated at Dulwich, he went on the stage in 1917. Quick to appreciate the opportunities offered by the New York stage, in 1920 he travelled to the United States where he spent his professional life until 1939. He soon gravitated towards Hollywood where, throughout the 1930s, he enjoyed starring roles in films which have since become classics, including *The Scarlet Pimpernel*, *Of Human Bondage*, *The Petrified Forest* and *Intermezzo*.

In 1939 his patriotic fervour led him to withdraw from Hollywood and return to Britain, where he found the film industry at a standstill. It says much for his ability and sheer strength of purpose that, instead of drawing to a close under these circumstances, his career took on a new lease of life.

Upon the outbreak of war he recognized his own propaganda value, particularly in terms of fostering Anglo-American relations through the medium of documentary film, an idea to which Whitehall lent only a deaf ear. A deal with Hitler still not being ruled out as late as the summer of 1940, the British had no desire to increase the level of government-sponsored propaganda. Howard did succeed in getting off the ground a more subtle venture, a feature film based on his 1935 success *The Scarlet Pimpernel*, with the plot updated and the action removed to Nazi Germany.

Pimpernel Smith was released in 1941, as was another famous anti-Nazi movie in which Howard had a starring role, Powell and Pressburger's *49th Parallel*. By this time Howard was broadcasting regularly to the United States in the BBC's 'Britain Speaks' series, much to the chagrin of William Joyce, 'Lord Haw-Haw', who broadcast what turned out to be perhaps no mean idle threats against Howard's life. Howard's series of unashamedly patriotic ventures continued with *The First of the Few*, released in 1942, in which he played R. J. Mitchell, the designer of the Spitfire.

Early in 1943, the sort of opportunity for which Howard had been angling since 1939 presented itself when the British Council invited him to lecture in the neutral countries of Spain and Portugal. Although worried about his likely reception in Fascist Spain, he agreed to the tour. Accompanied by his business partner, Alfred Chenhalls, he arrived in Lisbon on 28 April 1943. His lectures had no direct propaganda value, concentrating on such themes as his interpretation of *Hamlet* and his hopes and fears for the future of the motion picture industry. Chenhalls, however, was busy arranging for the distribution of Howard's war films and Howard himself was persuaded to personally present a showing of *Pimpernel Smith* prior to his departure for Spain.

As suspected, in Spain things were rather more difficult with pro-British activities being limited for the most part to the British Institute. During the course of his stay, one or two unsettling incidents occurred and his luggage was searched in his hotel room. Taking everything into account, however, the Spanish leg of the trip was quite successful, with Chenhalls once more entering into distribution arrangements for his partner's films.

On 20 May the pair left for Lisbon, where they spent the next week or so relaxing. A special screening of *The First of the Few* took place at the British Embassy on the evening of 31 May, a flight home being arranged for the morning of Tuesday 1 June. The flight selected was KLM 2L272; the aircraft, 'Ibis', was a DC3 capable of carrying up to 14 passengers. In order to accommodate Howard and Chenhalls, two passengers had to be removed from the passenger list, which was fully booked.

'Ibis' took off from Lisbon at 9.35am, climbing to a height of 9,000 feet. At 12.45pm she was over the Bay of Biscay, well north of Cape Vilano, when a squadron of German Junker fighters homed in on her. Without warning, they attacked and shot her to pieces. She managed to send a distress signal (received at Whitchurch) before her fuel tanks caught fire and she exploded in mid-air, her remains hurtling to the sea below.

The reaction in Britain was one of horror. The loss of Leslie Howard, both a popular personality and a valued ambassador, led to a furore with questions raised in Parliament about the lack of protection afforded to civilian aircraft. The Nazis were cock-a-hoop at the news that Howard had been killed, a euphoria later tempered by the realization that by shooting down an unarmed civilian airliner operating from a neutral country, they had done nothing to improve their reputation internationally. There followed shame-faced excuses to the effect that 'Ibis' had been mistaken for an enemy bomber.

Rumours flourished. Of some interest are the usual batch of premonitions, in this case attributed to Howard's fellow passengers. Kenneth Stonehouse, a Reuter correspondent, admitted to having a bad feeling about the flight, while an oil executive, Bill Shervington, had dreamt that the aircraft would be shot down. Howard himself had expressed a sense of unease at the prospect of the entire Iberian tour.

A further curious incident involved a Roman Catholic priest, Father Arthur Holmes, who was booked on the flight but who had to get off the plane, abandoning his luggage, as a result of an urgent summons to either the British Embassy or the Papal Nunciature (reducing the total number of passengers to 13). Enquiries later revealed that no one at either establishment had sent any such message, a mystery which has never been resolved. Did the message amount to a tip-off from someone who knew that 'Ibis' would be shot down?

Although the issue of the loss of the 'Ibis' revolved around Leslie Howard, there were other passengers on board who might have been the targets of a Nazi plot. It was claimed, for example, that Chenhalls, who bore a passing, if unconvincing, resemblance to Winston Churchill, had been mistakenly identified as the British prime minister by secret agents in Spain. A more likely Nazi target was a Jew, Wilfrid Israel, who had undertaken many dangerous missions into Germany to evacuate Jewish refugees. Another significant passenger was Ivan Sharp, Director of the United Kingdom Commercial Corporation, who had been negotiating important mineral export deals (to the consequent detriment of Germany). In sum total, Howard, Israel, Sharp and Shervington, whom the Nazis were convinced was a British secret agent, would have made a good catch.

Intriguing as these facets of the story may be, it is nonetheless a strong possibility that 'Ibis' would have been shot down with or without Howard or any of the others aboard. The Nazis were certainly worried about the activities of the British Council, the aim of which has always been to promote the attractions of the

110

British way of life. They were also concerned at what they considered to be the abuse of the principle of immunity, when civil aircraft were used to ferry to and from neutral countries those whose express purpose was to disseminate information hostile to the German war effort. 'Ibis' had already been attacked on 19 April when a squadron of Junkers opened fire on her. On that occasion she escaped by taking refuge in a cloud bank.

Examination of German war records failed to clarify matters. The Junker squadron's orders on 1 June included air-sea rescue and U-boat protection duties, although it seems likely that the brief was sufficiently wide as to allow for the destruction of any aircraft, suspect or otherwise, which strayed across its path.

In his book, *In Search of My Father*, Ronald Howard reminds us that no trace of aircraft or passengers was ever found. 'All one really knows is that physically he vanished, disappeared . . . into the blue.' And more than this, there is little that can with certainty be said.

10

BIRDS
OF A FEATHER

'Star Dust'

The Second World War was a time of great progress in aero-
nautics. Gone were the days of the struggling pioneers, individuals who endured official hostility and neglect, saving every
penny in order to put themselves in the air. By 1945 Germany
had developed a jet fighter and the deadly V2 long-range rocket,
while the United States had the atomic bomb with the technology to transport and deploy it. Already, far-sighted scientists
were beginning to gaze beyond the Earth's boundaries.

It came as no surprise, therefore, when the relatively straight-
forward matter of transatlantic airline travel was addressed in the
immediate post-war years. And who could be better qualified to
operate such routes than the veteran RAF bomber pilots? And
what more trustworthy aeroplane design to utilize than that
of the famed Lancaster bomber? So thought the founders of
the rather grandly named British South American Airways
Corporation.

BSAAC was formed by a group of ex-Pathfinders, the men
whose job it had been to go ahead on a bombing raid to identify
and illuminate the target for the night. The company had its
headquarters in Grafton Street, London W1 and these new
pioneers were affectionately known as the 'Grafton Street
Fifteen'.

The South American continent had managed to remain neutral
during the war, and offered much in the way of dividends to
enterprising investors for whom European post-war austerity

112

held little appeal. It was for such entrepreneurs that BSAAC aimed to cater.

BSAAC began life with Lancastrian and York aircraft. The route they flew was necessarily divided into stages: from London airport to Lisbon, and then on to the Azores, Bermuda and the West Indies. The final destination might be Cuba or Buenos Aires.

One of the early Lancastrians, christened 'Star Dust', had seen two years' service when, on 2 August 1947, she was waiting at Buenos Aires to take on board six passengers for Santiago – an additional internal service for which passengers would be transferred from one aircraft to another.

The crew of the 'Star Dust' were experienced, standard BSAAC material. Captain Cook, a much-decorated RAF navigator, had made many flights across the Andes. The first and second officers, together with the radio officer, were also RAF veterans. BSAAC had worked out three Buenos Aires – Santiago, trans-Andean routes: over Mendoza, the shortest route, but also the most hazardous with several towering Andean peaks in the way; to the north over San Juan, running back down to Santiago; and the the south, through the Planchon Pass – the safest route. It was always tempting to take the most direct route, and Cook made exactly that choice.

At 1.46pm 'Star Dust' took off from Buenos Aires with six passengers, five crew and six hours' worth of fuel. Her estimated arrival time was 5.31pm. For the first three hours the flight went smoothly, with regular radio contact maintained. At 5pm, upon receipt of information that cloud cover extended to 23,000 feet, Cook began the steep climb from 10,000 to 24,000 feet to attain clear skies. At 5.30pm estimated arrival time was adjusted to 5.45pm. Then, at 5.41pm, 'Star Dust' transmitted one mystifying word, 'STENDEC' – and disappeared for ever. A full-scale search, spearheaded by the Chilean Air Force, found no trace of the missing aircraft.

The mystery is two-fold. What happened to 'Star Dust' and what was the significance of the curious 'STENDEC' transmission? As far as the latter is concerned, it has been suggested that when translated into properly punctuated morse code the word represents the normal signing-off procedure which the radio operator would have used. This appears to be an absurdly simple explanation. Yet if true, it only deepens the real mystery, implying that, four minutes from landing time, there was nothing amiss with the flight. What sudden, completely unexpected catastrophic event could have occurred to render even the transmission of a distress signal impossible? And why, with the search area narrowed down to the near vicinity of Santiago, was no wreckage ever found?

A somewhat lame solution suggested by the enquiry into the mystery was that icing could have occurred. But, if icing was going to occur at all it would have manifested itself much earlier in the flight. In any case, such a theory fails to take account of the proximity of 'Star Dust' to Santiago airport.

The only way in which a crash hypothesis becomes feasible is for 'Star Dust' to have drifted off-course, and it is just conceivable that this is what really happened. Cook was flying above the cloud ceiling at 24,000 feet. Estimated arrival time had already been put back by 15 minutes because of strong head-winds. Having very little in the way of dependable navigational equipment, 'Star Dust' may have drifted off-course. The Lancastrian, moreover, was not pressurized, which in turn meant that the descent from 24,000 feet would have to be gradual. A slow descent through the cloud, starting at a point somewhat removed from the approach to Santiago airport, may well have come to a tragic conclusion on an Andean mountainside.

In August 1989 the remains of a jumbo jet which had disappeared 23 years before, in 1966, were discovered near the top of Mont Blanc. It is believed that the Boeing 707 crashed into the side of the 15,800-foot mountain, evidence from the human remains suggesting that the survivors had been forced to turn to cannibalism in a despairing effort to stay alive before expiring from a combination of injuries and the extreme cold. It is likely that such was the end of the 'Star Dust', her passengers and crew on 2 August 1947. Perhaps, some day, the Andes will yield up their secret.

'Star Tiger'

Although concerned at the loss of 'Star Dust', the men in Grafton Street viewed the incident quite objectively as a freak accident, a 'one-off' which would not affect the long-term future of BSAAC. They could not know that less than six months later another tragedy, with more far-reaching consequences for the company, would strike.

At the time of the loss of 'Star Dust', BSAAC were already seeking replacements for the ageing Yorks and Lancastrians. During the course of 1947 they took delivery of three Tudor IV aircraft which, like the Lancastrians, were closely related in design to the Lancaster bomber. One of these, 'Star Tiger', left London airport on 27 January 1948 on her own flight into oblivion.

'Star Tiger' had clocked-up almost 600 hours' flight-time and had recently been fully serviced. Her destination was Cuba, via Lisbon, the Azores and Bermuda. She carried six crew: Captain McMillan, first and second officers (all Pathfinder veterans), an experienced radio officer, Robert Tuck, and two stewardesses. The 23 passengers included Air Marshal Sir Arthur Conningham.

Despite the overhaul she had undergone, 'Star Tiger' began to experience problems even before reaching Lisbon with the breakdown of her heating system and trouble with one of her compasses. Repairs were effected during the overnight stop. Next morning one of the engines failed, delaying take-off for two and a half hours while this too was repaired. As soon as the aircraft was once again airborne both the heating and the compass packed-up for a second time. Nevertheless 'Star Tiger' landed safely on Santa Maria Island, which BSAAC treated as little more than a re-fuelling stop, the customary procedure being to fly on to Bermuda after a short break for both passengers and crew. On this occasion, however, due to a forecast of strong head-winds, a decision was taken to make an extended overnight stop.

Also temporarily resting in the Azores was a BSAAC Lancastrian freighter. The pilot, Frank Griffin, discussed the situation with Captain McMillan and he too decided to delay take-off until the following day. They decided on a joint flight plan. Griffin, in the freighter, would take off first and relay information on weather conditions back to 'Star Tiger' which would follow on an hour later.

The next day, 29 January, Griffin took off at 2.22pm, McMillan at 3.34pm. 'Star Tiger' was 1,000 pounds overweight, taking into account full fuel tanks, McMillan having made his famous remark, 'Fill her up to the gills', as though he were off to drop a couple of thousand pounds of high explosive on Cologne, rather than being about to embark on a 2,000-mile voyage over an empty ocean. According to the rules he should have shed either passengers or fuel. He needed the fuel and wanted to avoid the bad press which would ensue from abandoning part of his payload. Reasoning that the excess weight would soon take care of itself in terms of fuel consumption, he decided to stretch a point. His decision could have had no bearing on the subsequent loss of the aircraft, but it is important in so far as it demonstrates how the rules he himself, as one of the 'Fifteen' had helped to formulate, were often bent.

The head-winds encountered by the Lancastrian and the Tudor were much stronger than had been expected, putting back the estimated time of arrival by an hour. They were also sufficient in intensity to blow the Lancastrian freighter 68 miles off-course. 'Star Tiger' also veered off-course to the north, but the error was soon corrected. At 3.15am on 30 January, Bermuda obtained a radio fix which put her squarely on target for her goal. Griffin, one hour ahead, landed at 4.11am.

Another safeguard BSAAC had built-in to the South Atlantic route was an obligation on the part of radio officers to maintain contact with base fields through regular 30-minute transmissions. But in this also, a 'fill her up to the gills' attitude was prevalent. Throughout the flight this ruling was ignored by Radio Officer Tuck, with periods of from 45 minutes to an hour elapsing without any attempt to make reports. Therefore at 3.50am, after having heard nothing from 'Star Tiger' for 35 minutes, Bermuda saw no reason for panic. Once again, according to the rule-book, a state of emergency should have been declared after a radio silence of more than 30 minutes. In practice this was not feasible. The cavalier attitude of the 'Brylcream Boys' in the air put ground control in a very difficult position. If the rule-book were followed to the letter a state of emergency would have been declared at some stage during every flight. Valuable time was thus wasted in making further attempts to re-establish radio contact and in making frequency checks with other radio stations. It was fully an hour and a half before a state of emergency was finally declared. 'Star Tiger' had disappeared. An extensive air-sea search uncovered no clues to her fate.

Griffin's aircraft had reached Bermuda safely, yet 'Star Tiger' following only one hour behind had vanished without a trace – a disappearance all the more mystifying for the lack of any hint of a distress signal. The official enquiry could only describe the loss as 'baffling'. What external force could so completely overwhelm the aircraft as to prohibit even the transmission of a distress signal?

One might make vague references to the aircraft's in-flight faults – the failure of the cabin heating and the faulty compass. Certainly BOAC had rejected the Tudor IV design, although it is only fair to say that their reasons for doing so had been dealt with in terms of a number of modifications carried out before BSAAC took delivery. The enquiry did not ascribe the loss to any design fault. The engine failure at Lisbon was also considered, although it was recognized that the Tudor IV could remain airborne on three or even two engines. Perhaps the enquiry should have considered more fully the procedures carried out for the engine repair.

To effect the repair, the petrol cocks to two of 'Star Tiger's' fuel tanks had to be turned off. These two cocks could only be manipulated when the aircraft was on the ground. If the maintenance men in Lisbon, working against the clock, had neglected to turn on these cocks when their work was completed then Captain McMillan would have found himself without a fuel reserve at a critical juncture in the flight. If Radio Officer Tuck had been absent from his transmitter at the time McMillan turned over to his non-operational fuel tanks, the absence of an SOS message, with 'Star Tiger' ditching into the sea, could be explained. Flying as she was at only 2,000 feet, the end would have come very quickly. As the enquiry noted, a combination of human factors and the mechanical element might well have combined to overcome both man and machine.

'Star Ariel'

The financial year 1947–48 saw BSAAC make a small operating profit while the fledglings British European Airways (BEA) and British Overseas Airways Corporation (BOAC) made considerable losses. Yet criticism was levelled at BSAAC on the grounds that the loss of 'Star Dust' and 'Star Tiger' showed that the profit had been made through a policy of 'safety second'. The one thing BSAAC could not afford was another disaster following hard on the heels of the other two.

There is a faint possibility that the loss of both 'Star Dust' and 'Star Tiger' could have been avoided had there been a flight engineer aboard. In the interests of economy (hence the 'safety second' criticisms) the flight engineer's position had been dispensed with in order to increase the number of passengers. As a result the Tudor IV design was modified to allow for flight engineer accommodation. The Tudor IV thus became the Tudor IVB. BSAAC took delivery of a IVB, christened 'Star Ariel', towards the end of 1948.

On 13 January 1949 'Star Ariel' took off from Heathrow airport for Jamaica. The routine flight went without a hitch and she was back in Nassau on the return flight when her plans were suddenly changed. Another BSAAC Tudor, 'Star Panther', en route from Heathrow to Santiago in Chile, had developed engine trouble and was stranded in Nassau. It was decided to transfer her passengers and crew to 'Star Ariel' which would take them on to Jamaica. 'Star Ariel's' passengers and crew would continue their flight to London aboard 'Star Panther' once repairs had been effected.

'Star Ariel', with Captain J. C. McPhee, a further six crew and 13 passengers, took off from Bermuda at 8.41am. Estimated time of arrival in Kingston was 2.10pm. Fifty minutes after take-off McPhee reported that he was flying at 18,000 feet and that visibility was good. A few minutes later the radio officer reported that he was changing his radio frequency, signing off from Nassau, Bermuda, to establish contact with Kingston, Jamaica. 'Star Ariel' was never heard from again, having joined her sisters, 'Star Dust' and 'Star Tiger', in another flight into mystery.

The tragedy was that her last radio contact had been an

announcement of her intention to change radio frequency. Nassau thought that the aircraft was now in touch with Kingston, while Kingston, having heard nothing from 'Star Ariel', presumed that she was still working with Nassau. It was a chance in a million, but it had happened. One of the unsolved mysteries surrounding the disappearance was the reason for 'Star Ariel' wanting to change frequencies at such an early stage in her flight.

Even allowing for any misunderstanding, the people on the ground were incredibly lax. No attempt to contact the missing aircraft was made by anyone for more than four hours. At 1.52pm, a few minutes before her estimated time of arrival, Kingston contacted Nassau for information. At 3.05pm 'Star Panther', now back in the air, was asked to search 'Star Ariel's' route for any trace of wreckage, but it was not until 5.08pm, an astonishing two hours later, that an emergency was declared and a full-scale search initiated.

The problem was that there was no indication of where 'Star Ariel' could have gone down, although it seemed probable that it was within 30 minutes of her final 9.42am transmission, presuming that the 30-minute ruling was being adhered to. The search went on for several days in a gradually widening arc, but to no avail. 'Star Ariel' had vanished without a trace.

In some ways her disappearance was the most mysterious of them all, flying as she was with ample fuel, at a good height and in clear skies towards a string of inhabited islands. In later years the vague suggestion was made that complete electrical failure might have been responsible. Such an occurrence would certainly explain the very suddenness of the loss and why there was no distress signal.

The cumulative effect on BSAAC of the loss of three aircraft in two years was devastating. For both BSAAC and the Lancaster-designed aircraft it was the end. BSAAC was subsequently absorbed into BOAC and the Lancaster's offspring were never again permitted to carry passengers. It was a sad ending for both the company and the aircraft, men and machines for which a brave new world no longer had any need.

11

INTO THE BLUE

SS *Waratah*

Between the years 1980 and 1985 Lloyd's recorded a worldwide loss of 16 ships, totalling 400,000 tons and with the death of 400 seamen, in what were termed 'mysterious circumstances'. These vessels and their crews disappeared without a trace. In this technological age it is perhaps surprising that such unexplained losses can occur. Yet it is often overlooked that, as far as safety standards are concerned, the sea is lagging far behind the air. Ocean-going vessels carry no flight recorders; there is no 'black box' that makes it possible to check on what went wrong when a tragedy has occurred at sea. Maritime disasters are still subject to a kind of 'acts of God' mentality in the way they are viewed and assessed. It is doubtful whether a 'black box' would provide the answer on every occasion, although perhaps it would have shed some light on one of the most mysterious maritime disappearances of the present century: that of the SS *Waratah* in 1909.

The *Waratah* (named after Australia's national flower) was built on the Clyde in 1908 for the Blue Anchor line. It was one of a number of cargo-passenger liners specializing in speed, luxury and unsinkability – a myth which was to explode with the loss of the *Titanic* in 1912. Unlike the *Titanic*, however, her unashamed luxury was augmented with a surplus of lifeboats. On the other hand, unlike the *Titanic*, she had no radio.

Her captain, Josiah Ilbery, had more than 40 years' experience at sea as man and boy. Despite displaying a tendency to roll in bad weather, *Waratah* gained her Lloyd's certificate of sea-worthiness and embarked on her maiden voyage on 5 November 1908, bound for Australia, with 67 passengers travelling in luxurious accommodation above decks and 689 emigrants packed like cattle into the holds – not such a far cry, in principle, from the concept of the convict ships which had ploughed their way to the penal settlements over a century before.

She completed the voyage and the return journey successfully, with only one or two problems requiring minor repairs. She had not encountered any weather sufficiently severe to put her to the test.

Her second voyage began on 27 April 1909, her outward load comprising 26 cabin passengers and 193 emigrants. In Adelaide she exchanged her exclusively human cargo for 6,500 tons of farm produce and industrial raw materials, taking on 200 passengers for good measure. Leaving the South Australian capital on 7 July, she arrived unscathed in Durban on the 25th. From Durban she put to sea on 26 July for Cape Town on the next leg of her homeward journey with 92 passengers, 119 crew and additional cargo. On the 27th she was sighted by the steamer *Clan MacIntyre* about 100 miles north of East London on the east African coast. *Waratah* and the 211 souls on board her were never seen again.

When *Waratah* was first listed as overdue by 24 hours on 29 July, no great concern was felt. Nevertheless, by the first week of August, both merchant and Royal Navy vessels were out looking for her on the 600-mile coastline between East London and Cape Town along which she must have disappeared.

The search continued for five months and was not officially called off until 15 December, although unofficial sorties went on until well into the spring of 1910. This was because the missing liner had been provisioned for a full year. Although the contents of her larder would surely then be rather mouldy, it was argued by optimists that she could still be drifting aimlessly in unfrequented waters.

The public enquiry into the mystery opened on 16 December 1909. During its proceedings a considerable mass of 'evidence' of varying degrees of reliability was considered. In the first place, there were the fraudsters. It says little for human nature in some quarters that all tragedies bring forth their quota of hoaxes. Messages in bottles were a favourite ploy in maritime disasters. In the case of *Waratah*, bottled messages, the jetsam of sick minds, were still appearing as late as 1922.

There were also the claims of people who genuinely believed

they had sighted bodies in the vicinity of the liner's disappearance. Invariably these turned out to be nothing more than floating whale blubber. There were stories of white children, survivors of the wreck, being raised by African tribes, and there was the customary complement of clairvoyants who had 'seen' the vessel sinking in heavy storms.

By far the most curious psychic experience had occurred on board *Waratah* before she reached Durban. It took the form of a recurrent nightmare of one of the passengers, Claude Sawyer. In his nightmare a bloodstained man in armour arose from the depths of the ocean and called to Sawyer standing (in his dream) on deck. The figure, brandishing a sword in one hand and a bloodsoaked cloth in the other, cried out 'Waratah! Waratah!' before disappearing beneath the waves. Sawyer became so alarmed that he decided to leave the ship at Durban.

Clearly the dream was an expression of Sawyer's subconscious fears about the ship. Ever since leaving Australia he had been worried about the extent to which she pitched and rolled. Instead of riding the waves she seemed to be ploughing straight through them, taking on board considerable water in the process. Strangely enough, after disembarking at Durban, Sawyer had one more dream, in his hotel, on the night of 28 July – only this time he saw a massive wave sweep over *Waratah* and turn her turtle, following which she disappeared from view.

It is true that there were many people who shared Sawyer's doubts about the ship's stability. Some crewmen from her first voyage remarked about her permanent list, adding that when she rolled over she seemed to take far too long to right herself. In general it was the older, more experienced seamen who were critical.

The only person, it appeared, who had at no time expressed an opinion about the reliability of the vessel was her master, Captain Ilbery, who it seemed had never so much as broached the subject with anyone. Could it be that he had in fact raised certain matters with the owners and that they, anxious to avoid any criticisms, were suppressing the information? It seemed odd that Ilbery had never once commented on the seaworthiness of the ship to his employers.

Some very telling evidence was provided by a passenger from her first voyage, Professor William Bragg, holder of the Chair in

Physics at Leeds University. Unlike some, Bragg was able to offer an informed opinion. According to his reasoning *Waratah* had not the capacity to right herself whenever she rolled, a starboard list being apparent for several days at a time during the voyage. There was much additional evidence furnished by former crew members to the effect that the liner had been difficult to load in terms of getting the balance right. Several experienced crew from the maiden voyage were so worried about the permanent starboard list that they declined to sign on a second time.

The court found that in view of the adequate lifesaving equipment on board, there should have been survivors. As there were none, it seemed probable that *Waratah* had been overcome by a sudden freak gale which had turned her turtle. But it remains strange that no flotsam was recovered from the much-searched limited area in which she disappeared.

Waratah's builders had certainly been provided with a difficult specification as far as her design was concerned, and the necessity for speed in her construction – a contractual penalty clause obliged the builders to pay a £50 fine to the owners for each day delivery was overdue – meant that there remained insufficient time before her launch to work out the safest way to load her. This was a dereliction which became only too apparent when, in July 1909, she encountered testing seas for the first and last time.

USS *Cyclops*

The United States has her own complement of mysterious maritime disappearances in every way as inexplicable as that of the *Waratah*. The best known is that of the USS *Cyclops*, which disappeared within the Bermuda Triangle in April 1918.

Like *Waratah*, *Cyclops* was one of the great 'unsinkables', a 20,000-ton collier built in Philadelphia in 1919 and launched in May of the following year. Also like the *Waratah* she was found to roll and pitch badly on her maiden voyage. Her captain, a German called Georg Wichmann, had changed his name to George Worley in an effort to avoid much of the anti-German feeling that was sweeping the Western world in the years prior to the First World War. Although he was a dependable employee with much experience of colliers, the quality of his seamanship would later be called into question, while his crew, like most casual seamen who worked on these vessels, could be unruly.

It was the function of *Cyclops* to service the US fleet with coal, which she did efficiently enough under Worley's experienced tutelage. Following the entry of the United States into the war in 1917, it was expected that such a vessel would play a prominent part in the North Atlantic convoy runs. Perhaps because of his German descent (and unconcealed sympathies for the Kaiser), Worley and his ship were kept busy on the American side of the Atlantic.

Early in 1918 *Cyclops* was ordered to undertake a mission to deliver coal to Brazil, under cover of which she would return with a cargo of manganese ore, used in arms manufacture. She set sail from Norfolk, Virginia, amid sub-zero temperatures on 8 January and made good time to the Brazilian port of Bahia, where she supplied the warship USS *Raleigh* with coal before taking on board more coal herself and proceeding to Rio. At this time her steam power was severely curtailed by the loss of a high-pressure cylinder which blew up. At Rio she unloaded some coal and took on board the manganese ore – over 10,000 tons insured for $500,000. She also took on board a passenger, a German collaborator by the name of Gottschalk. At Bahia she acquired 72 navy personnel, bringing the total number of passengers and crew to 304.

On 21 February she left Bahia for Baltimore with an estimated time of arrival of 7 March. In Barbados she made an unscheduled stop, the reason for which is not clear. Worley wanted to take on 600 tons of coal. As she was already carrying 1,500 tons, this seemed odd. When the request was queried Worley put to sea without further ado. She was last seen by the passenger liner *Vestris* which passed her in mid-ocean a day later. After this she unaccountably and inexplicably vanished. Five days after her ETA in Norfolk she had still not appeared and an attempt was made to contact her by radio. After another five days had elapsed the navy initiated a search which went on until May. But not a trace of her or her crew could be found. Finally, on 1 June 1918, she was officially declared lost with all hands.

The blow to American prestige was enormous, *Cyclops* representing the navy's biggest single maritime loss. For this reason there was reticence in high places to admit that she had been lost at all and perhaps the search, when finally undertaken, was not quite as whole-hearted as it might have been. It was inconceivable that such a titan of a ship could be lost without trace. She would undoubtedly turn up sooner or later. Much effort was expended in attempts to make radio contact with her. Ships' radios were still something of a novelty and it was yet to be recognized that, while they could lend aid to a search for a missing vessel, they did not constitute an adequate substitute.

Very little in the way of investigation of the disappearance was undertaken until after the war because it was presumed that the vessel had been torpedoed by a U-boat. Examination of German war records revealed that this was not the case. The only other wartime action which might have accounted for her loss would have been collision with a sea-mine, but had this occurred she would still have had the opportunity to send out a distress signal before going down.

Any prize for silliest theory must surely have been awarded to the maritime journal which asserted that *Cyclops* had been dragged down to the ocean floor by a giant squid. Another suggestion, not quite as silly as it might sound, was that Captain Worley had sailed to a German port and handed the ship over to the enemy. Mention has already been made of Worley's German sympathies, while some of the crew were also of German descent. Add to this the presence of the collaborator Gottschalk, and Worley's attempts to take on additional coal in Barbados, mix thoroughly, and one has a successful recipe for sabotage. Again, German war records would have provided some evidence of this if it had occurred, while the propaganda value of such a coup would surely not have been ignored.

Another possibility, considered at the time, was that the crew had mutinied and seized the ship. Worley had certainly acquired a reputation as a disciplinarian, which doubtless rankled with the casual labour constituting the crew. To exacerbate the situation, several crew were under lock and key for serious misdemeanours, all of whom had nothing to lose and everything to gain by taking over the ship. This theory, of course, is dependent upon the likelihood of a small minority overpowering the majority, which included the 72 personnel taken aboard at Bahia.

The likely fate of *Cyclops* involved several factors which, although unrelated, spelled disaster when collected together. The first problem was Worley's questionable seamanship. He had been at sea for the better part of 30 years and had developed unfortunate eccentricities of character. He would take to wandering about the ship dressed only in his underwear and a bowler hat, which did little to inspire confidence in a rough and ready crew. His poor navigation skills had also been noted, *Cyclops* often being observed approaching a port from the direction of her ultimate destination. And there was scarcely a ship of the line replenished with coal by *Cyclops* which did not bear the scars of her visit in the form of dents to the hull.

Coupled with this is the subject of the seaworthiness of *Cyclops*. It has already been observed that with the loss of one steam cylinder she was reduced to limping home to port. In addition to this handicap there is the matter of structural defects. Marine designers have always believed that 'bigger is better' whereas seamen are superstitious where large vessels are concerned, much preferring to sign-on for duty in ships of more modest proportions. There is some evidence to suggest that *Cyclops*, like the fabled giant after which she was named, was too big for her own good. In some respects she resembled modern tankers, which have been described as cathedral-like in design. This means that if a fracture occurs in the superstructure there is nothing to halt its progress and the fracture continues through the superstructure until the vessel literally breaks in half. The collier's half-empty holds could have led to this eventuality.

A further possibility involves her holds which, although half-empty, were carrying a lot of weight in the form of manganese ore, implying that she was lying very low in the water. Had she been unevenly loaded, heavy seas could have swamped her, filling the holds and capsizing her in much the same way as the *Waratah* must have been overwhelmed. To make it viable this option requires the occurrence of stormy weather, and it has always been claimed that the weather at the time of her disappearance was calm. Recent research, however, has revealed that along the eastern seaboard stormy conditions prevailed when *Cyclops* was making her way up to Norfolk. If she was suddenly and violently overwhelmed in this manner then the tragedy must have occurred very close to home.

An interesting perspective on the mystery is gained by setting aside the *Cyclops* for one moment and tracing the history of ships from the same stable as the doomed collier, vessels built in the same period and to similar specifications. One of these, *Orion*, had her back broken during an Atlantic storm in 1925, while two others, *Proteus* and *Nereus*, vanished without trace in 1941 in the same way as *Cyclops* – presumed victims of U-boat assaults.

In the search for an explanation for the loss of *Cyclops* it would be reasonable to suggest a combination of factors including poor seamanship, poor design and poor weather, the most telling clue being the fate of her sister ship *Orion*. Undoubtedly *Proteus*, *Nereus* and *Cyclops* herself ended their voyages in a very similar fashion.

The Seven Hunters

One of the most mysterious maritime disappearances of the present century occurred not at sea but on land – which is not quite so unfathomable a conundrum as it might at first appear.

Twenty miles west of the Isle of Lewis in the Outer Hebrides lie the Flannan Isles, at one time known as the Seven Hunters. They are little more than rocks, the largest of them, Eilean Mor, measuring just 500 yards by 200. Not dissimilar in appearance they comprise sheer grey cliffs rising to a height of some 200 feet, capped with lush green grass. In the past, sheep were ferried over for the grazing. Apart from migrant sea birds, the isles had only one other inhabitant: Saint Flannan, who lived the life of a recluse in the seventeenth century. The ruins of the chapel he built for himself can still be seen on Eilean Mor.

During the course of the nineteenth century the rocks began to constitute something of a hazard for the increasing amount of coastal shipping and claimed several victims before the authorities were persuaded to build a lighthouse. The tower was sited on Eilean Mor and was opened in 1899 after four years of dangerous and painstaking work.

The structure was sited near the old chapel and was 75 feet high with a light sufficiently powerful to be seen 40 miles out to sea. Two landing places, one on the western edge and one on the eastern edge of the isle, were blasted out of the rock. Stairways were etched into the cliff face at each landing point and lifting gear had been installed. But it was a lonely place. There can be few habitations on earth quite so lonely as a lighthouse. The handful of lighthouses remaining in operation today are for the most part unmanned, their workings having lent themselves to the process of computerization. At the turn of the century, however, the lighthouse on Eilean Mor was manned by a staff of four on a continuous rota, each man doing a six-week shift followed by a two-week break. A steamship, *Hesperus*, visited the island once a fortnight.

On 6 December 1900 Joseph Moore left the island for his two-week rest period, leaving on duty his three colleagues, Donald McArthur, Thomas Marshall and James Ducat. Due to severe weather *Hesperus* was unable to return to the lighthouse until 26 December, a week later than scheduled.

above: The SS *Waratah*, which went missing off the east African coast in 1909. Despite a five-month-long search, no trace of either the ship or the 211 people on board were ever found.
below: Captain Bill Lancaster and Mrs 'Chubbie' Miller with the plane in which they made their unsuccessful attempt to become the first people to fly from Britain to Australia in 1927.

above: Donald Crowhurst in his boat *Teignmouth Electron* before setting out to compete in the *Sunday Times* round the world yacht race.
right: The last page from Crowhurst's log.

I am what I am and and I
see the nature of my offence

I will only resign this game
if you will agree that of
the next occasion that this
game is played it will be
played according to the
rules that are devised by
my great god who has
revealed at least to his son
not only the exact nature
of the reason for games but
has also revealed the truth of
the way of the ending of the
next game that

It is finished —

It is finished

IT IS THE MERCY

11 15 00   It is the end of my
            any game the truth
has been revealed and it will
by dam so my familly require me
to do it

11 17 00   It is the time for your
            prove to begin

I have not need to prolong
the game

It has been a good game that
must be ended at the
I choose I will play this game when
I will resign the
game 11 20 00   There is
no reason for humfu.

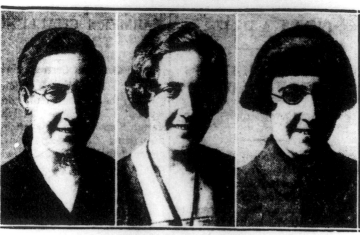

MRS. CHRISTIE DISGUISED.

Mrs. Agatha Christie as she was last seen (centre), and (on left and right) how she may have disguised herself by altering the style of her hairdressing and by wearing glasses Col. Christie says his wife had stated that she could disappear at will if she liked, and, in view of the fact that she was a writer of detective stories, it would be very natural for her to adopt some form of disguise to carry out that idea.

Agatha Christie's disappearance in December 1926 aroused great interest both in the media (*above*) and among the general public. The area around Newlands Corner, where her car was found abandoned, was one of many places searched by volunteers (*below*).

Although the trip was a routine one, Moore was concerned, partly because his companions had been forced to go without their Christmas mail and provisions, but more so because, for the previous few days, the light had not been visible. *Hesperus* made for the landing stage to the east of the island. Moore became increasingly worried when it became apparent that no preparations for the reception of the steamer had been made. Neither were any of the men in evidence. Under normal circumstances they would have been waiting eagerly, down by the landing.

A boat put out from the steamer for the landing stage and it was only with difficulty that Moore scrambled onto terra firma unaided. He made his way up the path to find the entrance gate and outside door to the lighthouse closed. The lighthouse was empty.

A thorough and systematic search revealed no trace of McArthur, Marshall or Ducat. Perhaps the most eerie aspect was the studied orderliness of the place. As in the case of the *Mary Celeste* there was no indication of panic. The wicks of the lanterns had been trimmed, the lens and machinery had been serviced, and the living quarters were neat and tidy. It was as if a giant hand had reached down from the heavens and plucked the three men out of the air.

One or two potential clues were found. The last entry in the log had been made at 9am on Saturday 15 December, so whatever mysterious event had occurred must have happened on that particular day. Subsequent evidence from coastal shipping confirmed that no light had been seen on the evening of 15 December. Much more important was the fact that both Marshall's and Ducat's oilskins and boots, which the keepers only wore when visiting the landings, were missing.

Although everything at the eastern landing point seemed to be shipshape there were traces of severe storm damage on the west side, the iron railings bordering the cliff stairway having been torn away in places. Could it be that Marshall and Ducat had, for some reason, both gone down to the west landing and, caught by a wave, been hurled into the sea? But why would they have visited the west landing? And how would this explain the disappearance of McArthur, whose oilskins remained intact inside the lighthouse?

According to the log, 12 and 13 December were days of strong westerly winds. On 14 December the wind dropped and it was still quite calm on 15 December, the day of the disaster. The mystery it seemed was insoluble, and it was some time before a possible scenario for the events of 15 December suggested itself.

When the three men disappeared the lighthouse had been operational for only a year. Later, when the base had become more established, it was noticed that on the west landing, in settled weather, the sea would suddenly and unexpectedly rise to an abnormally high level, assaulting the cliff face with all the ferocity of a tidal wave, to a height of 100 feet or more. Could it be that all three men, Marshall, Ducat and McArthur had ventured out, Marshall and Ducat dressed for work, with McArthur as observer, and that the sea had risen in such a fashion as to sweep them all to their deaths?

USS *Scorpion*

In the 1970s the editors of *Encyclopaedia Britannica* saw fit to include an entry on the Bermuda Triangle. Most of the information given was inaccurate, one debatable statement being that the 'most notable' disappearance in the region was that of the US submarine *Scorpion* in May 1968. If the disappearance is to be termed a Bermuda Triangle mystery (along with the *Mary Celeste* and Donald Crowhurst's *Teignmouth Electron*) then the area of the Bermuda Triangle must be extended out to the Azores, for it was at a point some 400 miles west of these islands that *Scorpion* disappeared.

Submarines have been lost by accident or error since the early nineteenth century. Leaving aside those sunk by enemy action, more than 100 were accidentally lost worldwide during the Second World War. Since 1945 only two dozen or so have been lost. By far the worst year was 1968, when three submarines disappeared in mysterious circumstances: the Israeli *Dakar* and the French *Minerve* in the Mediterranean, and the *Scorpion* off the Azores. Neither *Dakar* nor *Minerve*, which disappeared with 69 and 52 officers and men respectively, have ever been found and their fate remains open to speculation.

The *Scorpion*, launched in December 1959, was a vessel of 3,000 tons powered by a water-cooled nuclear reactor. Assigned to the US Sixth Fleet, she performed with great distinction in such naval exercises as she undertook. In February 1967 she entered the Norfolk naval shipyard, Virginia, for an overhaul. After that she successfully completed a number of post-overhaul sea trials. In March 1968 she was able to rejoin the Sixth Fleet on duty in the Mediterranean where she remained until May when, manned by a crew of 99, she set out on the return journey to Norfolk.

On 21 May, when 250 miles west of the Azores, she transmitted a routine progress signal which turned out to be the last contact she ever made. Estimated time of arrival was within one week of the progress signal. No immediate panic ensued when her arrival time came and went without sight of her, it being assumed that she was riding out rough weather in the Atlantic before coming in to dock. Efforts to establish radio contact with her proved futile, although maintaining communications with nuclear submarines always presents something of a problem due to the need for secrecy, which works to the disadvantage of any vessel that might run into difficulties.

At length *Scorpion* was reported overdue and a search was begun. When no trace of her was found, she was officially declared lost with all hands. During the course of continuing searches there were several false alarms. The remains of a submarine were located on the sea bed 100 miles off the Norfolk coast and it was thought at first that this must be *Scorpion* but, in the end, it turned out to be war wreckage dating from the 1940s.

A curious false lead concerned an intercepted radio message transmitted on 29 May and which gave *Scorpion*'s code name, 'Brandywine'. It was not possible to obtain an accurate fix on the supposed location of the call (not far from the position of the wartime wreckage) and it was eventually labelled a hoax. This seems odd, as the secret code names of nuclear submarines are not common knowledge, so the origin of the call has become a mystery in its own right.

In August 1968 a research ship, *Mizar*, claimed to have photographed and identified *Scorpion*'s crushed hull on the sea bed, 400 miles west of the Azores. This appeared to be quite a fortunate occurrence. In fact *Newsweek* magazine claimed that the US Navy possessed tapes recording the implosion of *Scorpion*'s hull, tapes which even contained a verbal message to the effect that the submarine was breaking up. In view of the staggering odds against *Mizar* stumbling by chance upon the remains in the course of her research activities, there do appear to be strong grounds for *Newsweek*'s claims (regarding which the navy saw fit to make no comment).

The fact that the submarine had 'imploded' (as opposed to having exploded) excluded the possibility of her having been sunk by a Soviet destroyer – one of the earliest rumours in circulation. The only really viable option was that some unknown, internal malfunction, mechanical or electrical – linked, perhaps, with human error – had led to the tragedy. Such were the findings of the court of enquiry. As the remains lay on the sea bed at a depth of 10,000 feet, it had not been possible to obtain pieces of the shattered hull for examination, and the court had before it only a series of photographs taken by *Mizar*.

The court was ready to point out that the crew was both

experienced and dependable, while *Scorpion* herself was in fine trim, largely due to her recent overhaul. Moreover, she had been the recipient of several efficiency awards during the early 1960s, although this must be qualified to some extent by the admission that the reliability of her surfacing systems was open to doubt. In addition, she was operating under a new commander, Francis Slattery, who had had only a short time to get to know the capabilities of his vessel and his men. Indeed, during her Mediterranean sojourn *Scorpion* had collided with a barge, though no structural damage seems to have occurred.

A section of the court's findings was labelled 'classified' and never released, indicating that public debate on matters relating to the submarine's construction and operation could have compromised the US defence capability, either through divulging secret information relating to submarine construction and operation or, alternatively, by exposing weaknesses within the nuclear-powered submarine fleet – weaknesses which could have constituted a considerable embarrassment as far as the principle of nuclear deterrence was concerned. For example, in 1973 USS *Greenling* came very close to sharing *Scorpion*'s fate. While on duty off Bermuda, as the result of a malfunctioning depth gauge, she dived to a hull-crushing depth and was on the point of imploding when the fault was noticed. This would, indeed, have been a mystery worthy of the Bermuda Triangle.

And what of the Bermuda Triangle apologists? Perhaps, they argued, *Scorpion*'s crew had been abducted by a UFO, in much the same way as the members of Flight 19, her empty shell being discarded, contemptuously, on the sea bed. Or had she been 'zapped' by an Atlantean laser-like death-ray, operating on the ocean floor? Or could she have disintegrated, having stumbled upon a parallel universe, her nuclear reactor in some way being responsible for an accidental journey which went horribly wrong?

No one is able to disprove claims that events took any of these turns. On the basis of information available at the present time, however, it seems highly probable that *Scorpion*'s loss resulted from a combination of human error and simple mechanical malfunction.

133

12

THREE OF A KIND

Raymond Hinchliffe

Commercial air travel was nothing new in the post-war years, but it had formerly been restricted to the well-to-do. The very smallness of aeroplanes in the inter-war years meant that airlines based their services on the provision of luxurious travel for the fortunate few.

One of the earliest civil airline pilots was Walter Raymond Hinchliffe, who chose to call himself by his second christian name rather than his first. In March 1928 Hinchliffe was working with British Imperial Airways, having been previously employed with the Dutch airline KLM and Instone Airlines. Like many of his colleagues Hinchliffe had been a First World War ace. During the course of his wartime exploits he had lost his left eye and wore an eyepatch to hide the disfigurement. His skill in the air was such that the civil airlines had had no qualms about employing him, although the enormous strain placed upon his remaining eye was beginning to tell and he had begun to worry about what the future might hold for him. But now, in the spring of 1928, there arose an opportunity which, if only he could grasp it, promised to set him up for life: he was introduced to a glamorous socialite, Elsie MacKay.

Elsie MacKay was the daughter of Lord Inchcape, the P&O shipping magnate. Multi-talented, self-assured and the richest heiress in England, she was a keen flyer. She was also very ambitious and had a notion to become the first woman to fly the Atlantic. And whatever Elsie wanted she always got – by hook or by crook. When, upon enquiry, she was told that Raymond Hinchliffe was probably the most outstanding pilot of his day, she decided that he must be the one to help her bring this, her latest dream, to fulfilment.

Over lunch at the Ritz, Elsie made Hinchliffe a very generous offer: £80 per month plus expenses, his own choice of aeroplane and all prize money if he would accompany her across the Atlantic. She even threw in a £10,000 life insurance policy as protection for his wife Emily and their two daughters. Hinchliffe thought the matter over very carefully. Only the previous year he had been involved in fruitless negotiations of a similar nature with an American, Charles Levine, and another heiress, Mabel Boll. Unlike Miss Boll, however, Elsie MacKay was an accomplished pilot in her own right, and this decided Hinchliffe in her favour. Elsie sent him over to the United States to buy a suitable aeroplane. His choice was a 200-horse-power Stinson Detroiter, the 'Endeavour'.

A difficult and unusual problem involving arrangements for the venture was the necessity for secrecy as far as Lord Inchcape was concerned. Despite her 34 years, had he known of Elsie's intentions he would have done all in his considerable power to prevent her carrying them out. So pains were taken to ensure that Elsie appeared only as financier, with Gordon Sinclair, a friend of Hinchliffe, being presented to the world as co-pilot.

Elsie persuaded the RAF to let her use Cranwell in Lincoln-shire as 'Endeavour's' starting point. This was essential as Cranwell possessed the only runway in Britain long enough to give the heavy Detroiter any chance at all of getting airborne.

The early days of March saw Hinchliffe, his wife, Gordon Sinclair and Elsie MacKay (complete with two chauffeur-driven cars) ensconced at the George Hotel in Grantham, making final preparations for departure. With money no object the team's plans were rather more rushed than one would have expected. Lord Inchcape was sniffing around and Elsie despaired of being able to keep up the pretence for much longer. Also, Hinchliffe had lost his job, Imperial Airways having refused to grant him leave of absence. And there was the worrying prospect that they might be pipped at the post by a rival German team which had set up camp in Ireland. Elsie was accustomed to being first, and the harassed Hinchliffe at last agreed, against his better judgement, to start on 13 March.

The weather forecast was atrocious that day but 'Endeavour' took off at 8.35am amid snow-drifts and a bitterly cold wind. At almost the last moment Hinchliffe tried to dissuade Elsie from accompanying him, but without success. Her ruse had worked. There was some suggestion of an easterly wind and, indeed, the wind did seem to be shifting around that way when 'Endeavour' struggled into the air. At 1.30pm she was sighted off Ireland and appeared, despite the early promise of easterlies, to be struggling against a head-wind. Further out in the Atlantic storm clouds were gathering.

All other factors being equal, they should have reached Newfoundland in 28 hours. 'Endeavour' had sufficient fuel for 40 hours, so Hinchliffe might even have headed for Philadelphia, with a view to setting a long-distance record. A lookout was kept on the Newfoundland coast, but a full day came and went with nothing being heard from 'Endeavour' or her crew. By 15 March it was clear that neither the aircraft, Raymond Hinchliffe nor Elsie MacKay would be seen again.

The month of March is traditionally the worst month of the year for air disasters. More fatal crashes occur in this month than in any other. In many cases severe air turbulence is the cause. The 'Endeavour', buffeted about amid the North Atlantic gales with a weary Hinchliffe at the controls, is not a pleasant picture on which to dwell. The aircraft had no radio (viewed by Elsie as excess weight), while such preliminary trials as the aircraft had undergone revealed both compass and fuel supply problems. In short, despite the protestations of success with which Hinchliffe punctuated his pre-flight conversations, it is hard to accept that a pilot of his considerable experience would have felt confident about undertaking such a perilous mission at such an inauspicious time.

Emily Hinchliffe at length applied to Lord Inchcape for her husband's salary, but the eccentric millionaire responded by freezing all Elsie's assets. To cap it all, the insurance company refused to pay out on the £10,000 insurance policy on the grounds that the premiums had not been properly paid. This must have seemed like the end, but in fact the strangest part of this tragic story with its bitter aftermath was only just beginning.

On 13 April Mrs Hinchliffe received a letter from a Mrs Beatrice Earl in Surrey. Mrs Earl dabbled in spiritualism and the occult in an effort to 'make contact' with her son who had been killed in the First World War. At the end of March, with this aim in mind, she was working in the comfort of her home with an ouija board. Instead of providing her with a consoling message from her son in the world beyond, for which she was searching, the instrument spelt out the following statement: 'I was drowned with Elsie MacKay', followed by: 'Fog, storm winds, went down from great height', and 'Off Leeward Islands. Tell my wife I want to speak to her. Am in great distress.'

Mrs Earl also wrote to the pro-spiritualist Sir Arthur Conan Doyle, who arranged for her to have a sitting with a leading medium, Eileen Garrett. Mrs Garrett also made contact with the deceased Hinchliffe, who seemed extremely vague as to what had happened to him. He could not say whether he had crashed during the day or night, but did state that 'Endeavour' had run out of petrol. 'Endeavour', though, had not been structurally damaged.

Conan Doyle then brought together Emily Hinchliffe and Mrs Garrett. Many meetings between the two women followed. The once-sceptical Emily, perhaps through her grief, was soon a convinced believer. As time went on, Hinchliffe, through Eileen Garrett's mediumship, provided more information about his disappearance. He spoke of having travelled about 900 miles before encountering very strong winds which broke 'Endeavour's' left wing strut. Making for the Azores with a faulty compass and oiled-up plugs, he was forced to ditch a mile from land. Hinchliffe himself was drowned while trying to swim ashore. Elsie MacKay had drowned in the cockpit.

It will be noted that this later information contradicted that given earlier in important respects. A particularly puzzling earlier statement was the one involving the Leeward Islands, suggesting that 'Endeavour' had gone down in the West Indies. The ingenious Conan Doyle interpreted the remark as meaning 'to the leeward of the Azores'. Towards the end of 1938 a wheel identified as belonging to the Detroiter was washed up on the County Donegal coastline, suggesting that 'Endeavour' had met her end en route to Newfoundland as opposed to near the Azores.

Notwithstanding the rather shaky evidence for his continued survival beyond the grave, Raymond Hinchliffe continued to prognosticate, becoming something of a spirit celebrity by predicting the *R-101* airship disaster.

Bill Lancaster

On 10 February 1962 a French army detachment was travelling across the open desert in southern Algeria when, at a spot about 40 miles west of the Trans-Sahara Road and 200 miles south of Zaouiet Reggane, it stumbled upon the mangled wreck of a light aeroplane. Huddled beside the wreckage were some well-preserved human remains. Tied to one of the wings was an equally well-preserved diary which not only explained the situation to the French but also solved one of the world's most mysterious disappearances.

Bill Lancaster had much in common with his fellow heroes and heroines of the air in the inter-war years. Having trained, like Raymond Hinchliffe, as a pilot in the First World War, he wanted to spend his life flying, but there was considerable competition for only a handful of openings. In 1927, however, his chance came when he was given an opportunity to become the first person to take a light aircraft from London to Australia.

Lancaster was accompanied on the flight by an adventurous Australian, Mrs 'Chubbie' Miller. Although they completed the flight their adventures en route included a crash in the Dutch East Indies, and the consequent delay led to their being overtaken by Bert Hinkler who took the record, the bows and the fiscal rewards, leaving Lancaster and Miller as the also-rans. They did get something out of it as, although both were married, they began an affair and set up home together in Florida soon afterwards.

By 1932, with Lancaster away from home for much of the time, scratching around for flying jobs, the gregarious Chubbie took up with a writer called Haden Clarke whom she had engaged to write her life story. Clarke was a neurotic character who appeared to live in a dream world of his own making. He asked her to marry him. With Lancaster out of sight (and apparently out of mind) she accepted and wrote to Bill to tell him the news. Outwardly, Lancaster gave no indication that he was unduly concerned. In reality he was deeply hurt, and when he returned to Miami he took a gun with him.

On the night of 13 April, upon his arrival in Miami, matters came to a head. Lancaster quite justifiably accused Clarke of going behind his back, and a full-scale row ensued. After dinner

138

things calmed down, at least on the surface. Clarke went so far as to assure Lancaster that he was 'the whitest man' he knew, a seemingly genuine if somewhat racialist observation.

This curious group then disbanded and retired to three different beds. In the morning only two were left alive, Clarke having been found shot through the head with Lancaster's gun. He had apparently left two suicide notes. When these were found to have been written by Lancaster, the airman was charged with murder.

Lancaster's defence was that, learning that Clarke had used Lancaster's gun to blow his brains out, the defendant realized that suspicion would fall on him so he had concocted the suicide notes to help confirm Clarke's action. Defence counsel managed to discredit Clarke's character, while Lancaster's was enhanced, largely through presentation to the court of his meticulously kept diaries which seemed to bear out his claims to be a man of honour. By the skin of his teeth, he got off.

Leaving Chubbie behind, Lancaster returned to England with another potential record-breaking flight in mind – from England to the Cape of Good Hope, a record held by Amy Johnson. For the attempt he chose an Avro Avian biplane previously owned by Sir Charles Kingsford Smith who was, like Lancaster, a former First World War ace and who was himself to disappear in 1935 during an attempt to fly from London to Australia.

In order to have any chance at all of clipping time off Amy Johnson's record, Lancaster had to cut directly across the Sahara desert from Oran to Gao, with a refuelling stop at Zaouiet Reggane, a total distance of about 1,500 miles and the most hazardous part of the journey. He took off from Lympne airfield in Kent on 11 April 1933 with some sandwiches and a thermos flask, for all the world as if he were setting out on a Sunday afternoon jaunt.

Over the course of the first stage of the flight, from Lympne to Oran, strong head-winds caused Lancaster to burn up much more fuel than he had planned for and so he made a refuelling stop at Barcelona. By the time he reached Oran he was already more than four hours behind Amy Johnson's time. He left Oran in the early hours of Wednesday 11 April, but several hours of night flying meant that he lost track of his position. He was in sight of the Trans-Sahara Road but by daybreak he did not know how far south he had flown. On seeing signs of a settlement he decided to land.

He landed not at Zaouiet Reggane but 100 miles to the north at Adrar, which he decided to substitute for Reggane as his refuelling stop. From this point, however, things began to go disastrously wrong. A sandstorm between Adrar and Reggane caused him to drift off-course and also made it necessary for him to stop at Reggane for yet more fuel.

Lancaster's chances of beating Amy Johnson's record were now gone, and with them his hopes of establishing himself on the international flying scene. Yet he still clung desperately to the thought of salvaging something by finishing the course. And it was in this state of desperation that he took off from Zaouiet Reggane at 6.30pm on the Wednesday evening. The sandstorm still raged and he had been advised to stay put.

In the early hours of Thursday 12 April, Lancaster was expected to land at Gao. But as the darkness gave way to light, it became apparent that he was not going to arrive. Throughout the day the authorities at Gao waited for him, but there was no escaping the fact that he had disappeared. A search was organized by air and by land along the Trans-Sahara Road, but to no avail.

Bill Lancaster would have been lost forever save for a chance happening 30 years later, when a French army patrol stumbled on the answer. His diary told the story. His engine had developed a fault just 150 miles south of Reggane. This explained why the search parties had failed to find him – they had expected him to be much farther south. He had crash-landed in the darkness and, although injured, had managed to survive for a full week by eking out his limited supply of water and by sheltering from the scorching heat beneath a crumpled wing. Using fabric torn from the aeroplane itself, he was even able to improvise flares. Doused in petrol, the strips burned brightly, but fruitlessly.

While the world advanced theories about his having committed suicide or being carried off by Bedouins, Lancaster had plenty of time to come to terms with his past. That he did so is borne out by the diary. During his trial for murder his diary had done much to save him. Now, in another hour of need, it came again to his aid as the sole companion to which he confided his innermost thoughts. Life had given him what he wanted: he had achieved immortality.

Donald Crowhurst

In many respects Donald Crowhurst resembled Bill Lancaster. Like Lancaster he was an adventurer, always in search of excitement and always managing to get into – and out of – scrapes. Like Lancaster he was looking for something more: he was a man in search of a mission. They were a generation apart, but both would have found fulfilment as fighter pilots in the Second World War. Yet, as fate would have it, Lancaster was born too early, Crowhurst too late.

Crowhurst was born in 1932, when Lancaster was planning his last flight. (In 1962, when Lancaster's remains were found, Crowhurst was setting up his own business, a gamble which led directly to his own ill-fated voyage.) A childhood in India was followed by a career in the RAF – until riotous behaviour forced him to resign his commission. A commission in the army followed the same pattern, after which he drifted from job to job in the electronics field before starting his own business, manufacturing navigation equipment. By the spring of 1967, when Francis Chichester sailed into Plymouth on completion of his round the world voyage, it had become clear that the business was failing.

In Chichester's achievement Crowhurst recognized the seeds of his mission: to sail around the world non-stop, thereby upstaging Chichester who had made a prolonged stopover in Australia. He had always been interested in sailing, which he had taken up seriously 10 years before. He owned a light sailing boat to which he would retreat from time to time. The problem with good ideas is that they always occur to many people simultaneously, and the prospect of a non-stop circumnavigation appealed to others, including Robin Knox-Johnston and Chay Blyth.

As if on cue, in March 1968 the *Sunday Times*, which had partly sponsored Chichester, announced a non-stop round the world yacht race. Crowhurst entered immediately. He had one difficulty: he lacked a suitable boat which, for a man approaching bankruptcy, might have amounted to an insurmountable obstacle. But with the effrontery which only he could muster, Crowhurst tried to skirt the issue by attempting to acquire Chichester's *Gipsy Moth IV*, about to be put on permanent display at Greenwich by the Cutty Sark Society which, not surprisingly, turned down his request. Undaunted, he persuaded Stanley Best, an investor in his failing business, to put up the money for a trimaran to be built to Crowhurst's specifications.

The 40-foot *Teignmouth Electron* was launched on 3 September 1968. It had cost some £10,000. The construction of such a vessel, capable of withstanding the rigours of a circumnavigational voyage, in under five months was a remarkable feat, although the finishing left much to be desired, as did Crowhurst's own organization of equipment and supplies. But time was pressing, the *Sunday Times* rules limiting departures to between 1 June and 31 October. Nearly all the other competitors had made early starts (Blyth and Knox-Johnston having got under way in June) but organizational problems meant Crowhurst did not depart until 31 October itself. He had no hope of being first home, and the likelihood of deteriorating weather conditions meant that he stood little chance of winning the additional prize for the fastest time. But he had already burned his bridges. It was too late now to call it off.

The first week saw Crowhurst making good progress. It also saw the results of a hastily planned voyage as *Teignmouth Electron*'s deficiences came to light. Unreliable self-steering equipment, leaking hatches, inadequate pumping arrangements and faulty electrics were just a few of the problems which beset him. All could have been rectified had there been opportunity for adequate sea trials. The tight deadlines had allowed even the best organized competitors little chance to make adequate preparations for a nine-month sea voyage. An autumn announcement providing for departure dates commencing the following spring would have been a more responsible approach.

The second week involved several delays and only limited progress for Crowhurst, bringing his total mileage to a meagre 800 out of the full 30,000 of the voyage. During the course of his third week at sea, Crowhurst seriously considered throwing in the towel at Madeira before again reminding himself that admission of failure was not for him a viable option – especially as an alternative plan began to formulate in his mind.

From the fourth week the entries in Crowhurst's log became much sketchier, comprising only broad hints as to his actual position. They were coupled with a jubilant claim on 10 December to have sailed 243 miles in a 24-hour period, thereby setting a new record for a lone yachtsman. The skills of his press agent ensured maximum news coverage, with only a handful of spoil-sports (including Chichester) expressing reservations about the validity of the claim.

Crowhurst now launched himself into the laborious chore of maintaining two logs – one charting his real progress, the other his fictitious progress, the latter requiring a tremendous degree of skill and application. The essence of his master plan was to follow a hovering course along the South American coastline while plotting a fictitious route around the Cape of Good Hope and on to Australia and the Pacific. The trick was to co-ordinate the two so that he took up the fictitious log at the time when he would have expected to be rounding Cape Horn on the homeward run.

Christmas came and went. He had plenty to keep him busy. Apart from the gargantuan task of plotting his fictitious course and presenting it in a convincing manner in the log, there was a need to keep a constant lookout for ocean-going steamers for fear that *Teignmouth Electron* might be recognized. There was also a possibility of a radio-fix identifying her true position, which Crowhurst dealt with by hinting at generator trouble and main-taining radio silence for 11 weeks. A third, more serious problem, was the need to dock for essential repairs. Crowhurst put into a small estuary on the Argentinian coast. There, at the little settlement of Rio Salado, the repairs were completed. But he had taken a terrible risk. Although no one at Rio Salado knew of the race, under the rules of which Crowhurst would have been disqualified for docking en route, the local coastguard did log the fact that *Teignmouth Electron* had put in there.

Nevertheless, Crowhurst pressed on with his grand deception, breaking radio silence on 11 April to announce that he had rounded Cape Horn, but failing as always to give an exact position. Finally, on 4 May, he decided it was time to re-enter the race. By this time there were only two survivors, the little-fancied Robin Knox-Johnston and Nigel Tetley (also competing in a trimaran), both of whom had rounded the Cape and were sailing on up into the Atlantic. The spotlight was on all three, with Knox-Johnston poised to win and Crowhurst tipped to make the fastest time.

After much deliberation Crowhurst decided to let Tetley achieve the fastest voyage time. In truth, he was becoming increasingly concerned over the ability of his log to withstand the close scrutiny it would certainly undergo if he took the prize. He calculated that the fame and fortune accruing to him from the achievement of having stayed the course would set him up nicely. Unfortunately, Tetley's boat *Victress* sank on 21 May.

Crowhurst, short of sinking himself, must now go on to make the fastest time and have his log scrutinized by Chichester. It is from this point that the log displays a growing irrationality, the sum total of the entries amounting to a rambling metaphysical discourse with Crowhurst, in some obscure way, identifying himself with God and the cosmos.

On 10 July *Teignmouth Electron* was spotted by *Picardy*, a packet en route from England to the Caribbean. She appeared to be drifting aimlessly. As there was no response to *Picardy*'s efforts to attract attention, an investigation was made. The situation encountered was eerily reminiscent of the *Mary Celeste*. The trimaran seemed to be in good trim with her equipment in reasonable order, although the cabin was disorganized and the chronometer was missing. The log-books were intact.

Teignmouth Electron was hauled on board *Picardy* and a futile air-sea search was organized, with Crowhurst's family hoping against hope that he might still be alive. But within a week of the trimaran being found the log-books had told their tale, which led to the inescapable conclusion that Crowhurst had committed suicide. His mind unbalanced, and knowing that his fraudulent log could not bear scrutiny, he had thrown himself overboard. There are other possibilities, of course. There have been several unverified sightings of Crowhurst since his disappearance, from England to the Cape Verde Islands, and unsubstantiated claims that he is living in places as far apart as South America and the Azores. Or perhaps he simply fell overboard?

Like Bill Lancaster, Donald Crowhurst was the stuff of which heroes are made. That the world had no use for a man of his outstanding abilities should not result in his condemnation. In the final analysis his voyage must be seen as a success in that, as with Lancaster, he achieved the fame he craved, albeit at the cost of his life.

13

LOST AND FOUNDLINGS

Kaspar Hauser

As we have seen, it is difficult enough to arrive at satisfactory explanations for the countless mysterious disappearances on record both throughout the ages and throughout the world. How, then, can we account for something even more mysterious – the inexplicable 'appearances' of men, women and children? For it is an inescapable fact that people occasionally turn up where we know they ought not to be.

The most celebrated case of an unexplained appearance is that of a German youth, Kaspar Hauser, who turned up in Nuremberg in May 1828. When first seen he was wearing a grey riding outfit and a pair of old boots, and brandished a letter addressed to a captain of dragoons stationed in the town. The letter was purportedly written by a labourer with 10 children who claimed to have received the boy in 1812 and had kept him shut up in his house for the following 16 years. He now found that he could keep the boy no longer and was sending him to the captain to see what, if anything, could be done with him.

The boy appeared to the captain to be little more than an imbecile, capable only of monosyllabic grunting. The police, to whom the captain applied for advice, took a less than constructive approach to the problem by throwing the hapless youth into prison. Managing to acquire a pencil and paper, he wrote down the name 'Kaspar Hauser', although he failed to identify with it personally.

News of his arrival spread throughout the city and he became something of a nine days' wonder, people flocking from far and wide to catch a glimpse of him. He was under-developed physically, being under 5 feet in height with small, delicate hands and feet, and mentally displaying behaviour more appropriate for a babe in arms. After spending two months being treated both like a common criminal and a public sideshow, Kaspar was taken care of by a Professor Daumer, an educationalist and philosopher who introduced him into his household and attempted to discover something of the boy's past.

Having exchanged the role of public spectacle for that of anthropological specimen, Kaspar Hauser displayed remarkable speed in the process of recall and the assimilation of new knowledge. According to the information he supplied, he had been kept a prisoner throughout his short life in what was little better than a dark hole, where he sat on straw on the ground. While he slept, bread and water were brought to him and he was supplied with clean linen. Not until an unidentified man visited him during his waking hours and taught him to walk, shortly prior to his arrival at Nuremberg, did he have knowledge of any human contact.

His behaviour was certainly suggestive of long imprisonment and deprivation. He displayed no fear of fire, once thrusting his hand directly into a flame. In addition to being able to see remarkably well in the dark, he was heavily dependent upon his sense of smell for discerning objects at a distance. For over a year Professor Daumer persevered with him, encouraging him to develop skills other than the use of his senses. He made good progress in providing his charge with an education, until the cataclysmic events of 17 October.

It was upon this day that Kaspar Hauser was discovered senseless in the cellar of Daumer's house. Bleeding heavily from a wound in his forehead, he was put to bed where he remained for some days. At length he was able to give a sketchy account of what had happened. It appeared that he had been assaulted by a masked man, who had then run away, after which Kaspar had taken refuge in the cellar – a hiding place which, as a result of his childhood experiences, seemed a natural choice.

Thenceforth he was moved to the house of a magistrate and put under police guard. In June 1830 he was again moved, this time to the more congenial surroundings of a Nuremberg businessman by the name of von Tucher. He was sent to the local grammar school where he proved an adept pupil, despite which there were only modest long-term plans to apprentice him to a bookbinder.

In 1831 new hope dawned for his future prospects in the personage of Lord Stanhope, the celebrated English eccentric then on a visit to Nuremberg. Kaspar was still very much an object of pilgrimage for visiting dignitaries, and Stanhope thought he might make quite an amusing addition to his entourage, taking him on a grand European tour. He even intimated that he might consider formal adoption. Unfortunately, Kaspar's expectations carried the seeds of his own destruction, for Stanhope encouraged him in the belief that he was of royal blood, a rumour which developed into the belief that Kaspar was the rightful heir of Charles, Grand Duke of Baden. Through a complicated web of intrigue – a feature of court life in the conglomerate of principalities which we now know as Germany – Kaspar, so it was claimed, had been cruelly cheated of his inheritance. His case gained some credibility when he met the Grand Duke's sister, Queen Caroline, who insisted that there was a strong family resemblance. Contemporary portraits seem to bear this out.

The immediate result of this theory was that Kaspar began to entertain delusions of grandeur. In 1832 Stanhope took him away from Nuremberg, settling him in Ansbach under the care of a protestant minister, Dr Mayer. It was believed that this would be only a temporary arrangement while Stanhope finalized his plans to take Kaspar to England, but as with many mortals before and since, Kaspar discovered how unwise it was to put one's trust in 'princes'. Before long, Stanhope grew tired of his new pet; the novelty value having worn off, he abandoned him completely to Mayer's care.

Mayer was not the most enthusiastic of Kaspar's supporters. He was suspicious of his story of the early years of confinement, accusing him both of laziness and deceit. Kaspar's cup of woe seemed replete when he was put to work as a government clerk, copying manuscripts. He took heart in making plans for the day when he could return to Nuremberg and his friends. But such was not to be his fate.

On 14 December 1833 during the late afternoon, Kaspar staggered into Dr Mayer's house, holding his side. As far as

Mayer could tell, Kaspar had been walking home through a public park when he had been accosted by a tall, dark stranger dressed in black, who handed him a purse and stabbed him when he opened it. The purse was found to contain a note – written backwards in pencil – in which the mysterious assailant had given a clue to his identity, indicating that he came from the Bavarian border and that his name was 'M.L.O'.

The stab wound did not, at first sight, appear to be particularly serious. Kaspar's recovery would today have been assured, but primitive early nineteenth century surgery left much to be desired and he sank into a fever and died three days later. The mysterious 'M.L.O' was never traced.

As will happen in such cases, arguments raged between Kaspar's supporters and his detractors as to his credibility. The detractors believed that he had been merely a young beggar who had cooked up the story about his early imprisonment. His strange behaviour, they claimed, was nothing more than a sly imposture geared to winning him a life of ease. His supporters argued for the conspiracy theory – that he was indeed of royal blood, and that certain influential people, alarmed at the attention he was attracting, felt a need to silence him.

In favour of the critics, it has to be said that both the attacks upon Kaspar (including the earlier one while he was in the care of Daumer) resulted in wounds of a type which led some people to believe that they might have been self-inflicted. Both alleged attacks occurred on occasions when interest in him appeared to be on the wane.

Others have broadened the scope of the debate in suggesting that he was a visitor from another time, or perhaps from another planet. A large reward failed to turn up any further information about Kaspar or his murderer – if there ever was a murderer. His epitaph sums up all that can, with certainty, be said of him: 'Here lies K H, the riddle of the age. His birth was unknown, his death mysterious.'

Count St Germain

If the story of Kaspar Hauser has no beginning, at least it does have an end. The story of Count St Germain, however, is one that has neither beginning nor end.

The self-styled 'Count' St Germain, like Kaspar Hauser, arrived from nowhere on the European scene. Many unfounded rumours as to his origins were in simultaneous circulation: he was the illegitimate offspring of the royal house of Spain; even more romantically, his pedigree had its roots in the principality of Transylvania, home of vampires and werewolves. But where he came from was of little consequence, as all attention was focused firmly on what he claimed to be able to do.

Primarily he was an alchemist, claiming to hold the secret of how to turn base metals into gold. Alchemy was essentially a pseudo-science appertaining to the Middle Ages. By the early eighteenth century when St Germain first came to public notice, it was a forgotten skill (assuming the concept to have had any validity in the first instance). Yet largely through the efforts of St Germain and a contemporary charlatan called Cagliostro, it enjoyed a brief Indian summer of popularity in the Regency era.

St Germain's second claim to fame rested on the apparently irrefutable evidence, supplied by his own physical appearance, that he had discovered the secret of eternal youth. His alchemical skills were so polished, not because he had studied the works of the medieval masters of alchemy such as Flamel, Albrecht and von Hohenheim, but because he had himself been a practising alchemist in medieval times! On one occasion he was recounting a conversation he said he had had with King Richard I at the time of the Crusades, when he turned to his servant for verification of one or two details. The servant's response was that he was unable to say one way or the other as he had been in his master's service for only 500 years.

Some proof of St Germain's longevity is provided by the Countess von Georgy who met him in the year 1710 when, she noted, he appeared to be in his mid-40s. Over half a century later the countess, then in her 70s, met him again and was amazed to discover that he seemed to be no older. Twenty years later he was still going strong, an active participant at the court of Louis XVI and Marie Antoinette.

As far as his many talents are concerned, he was a brilliant musician and composer, his wit and conversation were unsurpassed, his fount of political and philosophical knowledge was inexhaustible, and he possessed many psychic gifts such as precognition and the ability to indulge in astral travel at will. He certainly accomplished much in the way of down to earth travel. Throughout the eighteenth century, as well as travelling extensively in western Europe, he is recorded as being seen in Russia, Persia, India and North Africa – and this in an age when journeys were arduous and daunting prospects.

Whatever he wanted to do and wherever he wished to go, expense was no object. His wealth was unparalleled. As well as the transmutation of base metals into gold, he was able to manufacture one large single diamond from several small ones and could also make pearls grow to a spectacular size. Virtually every major royal house in Europe was his patron at some time or another. In France he was supplied with laboratories to enable him to further his alchemical studies, while in Venice he had a factory which capitalized on his own process for turning flax into silk.

The fact that he could move quite easily among the world's ruling dynasties led him inexorably into the field of international espionage. He was instrumental in furthering the efforts of Louis XV to bring to an end the Seven Years' War with England, and he played an important covert role on the side of Russia in her war with Turkey a few years later. It was claimed that his sympathies had always rested with Russia, and that he had actually been working as a double-agent for the Russians during the time he spent at the French court of Louis XV. St Germain's penchant for interfering in politics led to his arrest, on charges of spying, in England in 1745. He was accused of involvement in the Jacobite rebellion, but after questioning was released. His experience did not alienate him from the British, however, and he visited England again 15 years later.

The year 1779 saw St Germain living in Germany under the patronage of Prince Charles of Hesse-Kassel, with whom he worked at alchemy to the mutual advantage of both. And then in February 1784 something odd occurred: the death of St Germain. He was provided with a grave and a tombstone, the event being marked with an appropriate entry in the parish records. The tombstone, erected by Prince Charles, bore the following inscription: 'He who called himself the Comte de Saint-Germain . . . of whom there is no other information, has been buried in this church.' It may be notable, in light of what followed, that no mention was actually made of death itself.

St Germain's supposed death did not appear to curtail his globe-trotting existence. In 1785 he appeared at an occult conference in Wilhelmsbad and in 1788 appeared in Versailles, where he predicted to Marie Antionette the outbreak of the French Revolution a year later. In 1789 King Gustavus of Sweden reported that St Germain had visited him to warn of impending danger (Gustavus was then planning a coup d'etat to strengthen his position). From time to time St Germain also visited the diarist Mlle d'Adhemar, who noted that he looked as youthful as ever. Further appearances have been recorded down to the twentieth century. In 1972, for example, a Parisian claiming to be none other than the count himself appeared on television and performed the ultimate alchemical feat, turning lead into gold.

As with Kaspar Hauser, so St Germain had his supporters and a no less vehement army of detractors. To those who were jealous of his success in court circles he was a charlatan and a rogue, and many scurrilous tales were undoubtedly circulated by his piqued rivals for royal favour. His most ardent admirers accepted him for what he claimed to be – the supreme alchemist who had discovered both the means of the transmutation of metals and the secret of eternal life. Perhaps, on the occasion of his next scheduled appearance, he can be asked to clear up the mystery.

Agatha Christie

In early December 1926 a well-dressed young woman of means, calling herself Theresa Neele, was staying at the Hydropathic Hotel in Harrogate. She had, she said, recently arrived in Britain from South Africa. She was a very pleasant person, mixing well with the other guests and, like them, taking an interest in the major topic of conversation: the disappearance of the woman writer of mystery stories, Mrs Agatha Christie.

Agatha Christie was one of those people whom it is hard to imagine as youthful. She is fixed in the public image as a large, over-dressed, matronly woman with white hair and the appearance of comfortable pleasantness which comes with age – very similar in looks to the actress Margaret Rutherford, who played Mrs Christie's celebrated detective, Miss Marple, in the cinema.

Agatha Christie was born Agatha Mary Clarissa Miller in Torquay in 1891. A cosseted childhood and an inadequate formal education did little to provide her with adequate preparation for taking life's knocks. Her secure, middle-class upbringing was something on which she later looked back with an increasing, aching nostalgia. With the death of her father when she was only 11, life became more materially difficult, although she was protected from the vagaries of the outside world in the family home, Ashfield, for which she retained a lifelong affection.

She claimed that she began to write detective stories as the result of a bet between herself and her sister Madge, who laughingly proclaimed that Agatha lacked the imagination to do so. The tale is probably apocryphal, but it is the sort of thing readers of biographies love to hear. It is far more likely that she became a writer to earn money to help support her mother and herself and her husband.

In 1914, shortly after the outbreak of the First World War and following a whirlwind courtship, Agatha married a dashing subaltern, Archibald Christie. Like many couples at the time, they were under much strain to make ends meet, particularly as neither of them, by virtue of their backgrounds, could envisage life without servants. An additional literary income would therefore come in very useful.

With the coming of peace in 1918 Agatha gave birth to a daughter, Rosalind, and her first novel, *The Mysterious Affair at*

Styles. In the following years up to 1926 she published some half a dozen detective novels but did not make a great public impact.

During the spring of 1926 her mother died. Agatha travelled alone to Ashfield, where she shut herself away to relive her childhood memories. In her autobiography, published in 1977, the year after her own death, she remarked that she was so devastated after her mother died that she was unable to remember her own name when it came to signing cheques.

The death of her mother was not the only blow fate had in store for her. The neglected Archie had travelled down to Ashfield and, once there, announced that he had fallen in love with a colleague's secretary, Nancy Neele, and that he wanted to marry her. Agatha refused to believe it. Friends advised her that this was a phase all husbands went through at some time or another. But Archie subsequently moved out of their Sunningdale home while Agatha retreated still further into her shell.

On 3 December 1926 matters came to a head. On what was a bitterly cold evening, Agatha walked out of the house with only the clothes she was wearing and with only a few pounds in her possession, and drove away in her bottle-nosed Morris Cowley.

Next morning the abandoned car was found at Newlands corner, a Surrey beauty spot in uncomfortable proximity to a chalk pit and close to the Silent Pool. (The Silent Pool is, in fact, composed of two secluded pools, one of which is particularly dark and has the reputation of being bottomless and haunted by the ghost of a peasant girl drowned there in early medieval times.) The police, fearing the worst, had the pool dragged. Had she committed suicide? Or had Archie, despairing of gaining the divorce he wanted so badly, lent a hand? The plot thickened when Archie's brother, Campbell Christie, said he had received a letter from Agatha, posted in London on 4 December.

Although the head waiter at the Hydropathic Hotel in Harrogate knew little of Mrs Christie's background, he was particularly observant – much more so than the guests or the rest of the staff – and noticed a marked resemblance between the photographs of Agatha published in the press and Theresa Neele, the single lady from South Africa. The more he thought about it the more he became convinced that Agatha Christie and Theresa Neele were one and the same person. Ultimately, on 14 December, he put his job on the line and phoned the police.

Archie Christie arrived in Harrogate the same day. He discovered Agatha at dinner, reading a newspaper containing her own photograph. Theresa Neele was, indeed, Agatha Christie. Although she affected not to recognize him, the long-suffering Archie bundled her out of the hotel and patched up a story ascribing her extraordinary behaviour to amnesia. However, the difficulties she had experienced in signing cheques correctly must have abated sufficiently to enable her to procure the funds necessary for her stay at the Hydropathic, while it is inconceivable that the likenesses of herself in the newspapers she read were so poor that she failed to relate to them.

Indeed, critics of the escapade claimed that it had been nothing more or less than an elaborate hoax, an artfully contrived publicity stunt. In combing the countryside, they said, the police had run up a bill of several thousand pounds, which caused something of an outcry among Surrey ratepayers.

Was it a case of genuine amnesia or simply a gigantic fraud? As is so often the case, the truth of the matter probably lies somewhere between the two extremes. The evidence suggests that it is extremely unlikely that Agatha Christie was suffering from amnesia *per se*. On the other hand, such a vulgar means of gaining notoriety would have been completely out of character. It is much more likely that, being ill-equipped to deal with her husband's infidelity, she had just walked away from it, taking refuge in a contrived anonymity, an acerbic touch being provided by her use of the 'other woman's' surname.

The plot of the feature film *Agatha*, starring Dustin Hoffman and Vanessa Redgrave, did little to shed more light on the real-life mystery. In the movie, Agatha followed Nancy Neele to the Hydropathic Hotel with the intention of concocting a devilish scheme to murder her, only to apply it to herself in a horrific suicide bid.

In reality, Agatha gave Archie his divorce, enabling him to marry Nancy Neele. Later, Agatha herself remarried. Her second husband, the archaeologist Max Mallowan, was 15 years her junior. Although the marriage was a happy one by all accounts, there was very little in the way of passionate commitment. The easy-going Max was content to play second fiddle to his self-centred wife, while Agatha herself summed up her own feelings in the statement that if you have trusted people once and been let down, you do not feel inclined to commit your trust again.

One might almost say that everyone, after a fashion, lived happily ever after. Agatha's career as a writer took on a new lease of life as a result of the publicity attendant upon her disappearance. Even the wrath of the Surrey ratepayers subsided when they learned that the cost of the police investigation had amounted to only £25, as opposed to the original estimate of thousands. As for Agatha herself, she refused to discuss the subject. Her autobiography disappointed all who had hoped for the definitive explanation of the incident. Instead she dismissed it with an oblique reference to 'a strand in the tapestry of my existence. I must recognize it because it is a part of me. But there is no need to dwell upon it.'

FURTHER READING

General
Brett, Bernard *The Hamlyn Book of Mysteries* (Hamlyn, 1983)
Canning, John *Great Unsolved Mysteries* (Arthur Barker, 1974)
The Complete Books of Charles Fort (Dover, 1974)
Furneaux, Rupert *The World's Most Intriguing Mysteries* (Odhams, 1965)
Hitching, Francis *The World Atlas of Mysteries* (Pan, 1978)
Kingston, Jeremy *Mysterious Happenings* (Aldus, 1979)
Wilson, Colin and Damon *The Encyclopedia of Unsolved Mysteries* (Harrap, 1987)
Mysteries of the Unexplained (Reader's Digest, 1982)
The Unexplained (13 vols, Orbis Publishing, 1983)

Disappearances
Begg, Paul *Into Thin Air* (Sphere Books, 1981)
Churchill, Allen *They Never Came Back* (Ace Books, 1960)
Harrison, Michael *Vanishings* (New English Library, 1981)
Hayman, LeRoy *Thirteen Who Vanished* (Julian Messner, 1979)
Nash, Jay Robert *Among the Missing* (Simon & Schuster, 1978)

Chapter 1
Beattie, Owen and Geiger, John *Frozen in Time* (Bloomsbury, 1987)
Cummins, Geraldine *The Fate of Colonel Fawcett* (Aquarian Press, 1955)
Fawcett, Lt-Col P.H. *Exploration Fawcett* (Hutchinson, 1953)
Maufrais, Edgar *In Search of My Son* (William Kimber, 1957)
Younghusband, Sir Francis *The Epic of Mount Everest* (EP Publishing, 1974)

Chapter 2
Lockhart, Robin Bruce *Ace of Spies* (Hodder & Stoughton, 1967)
Pugh, Marshall *Commander Crabb* (Macmillan, 1956)

Chapter 3
Carew, Tim *The Royal Norfolk Regiment* (Hamish Hamilton, 1967)
Frere, Sheppard *Britannia: A History of Roman Britain* (Routledge & Kegan Paul, 1987)
Lacey, Robert *Sir Walter Raleigh* (Weidenfeld & Nicolson, 1973)

Chapter 4
Marnham, Patrick *Trail of Havoc* (Viking, 1987)
Moore, Sally *Lucan* (Sidgwick & Jackson, 1987)

Chapter 5
Clark, David *Labour's Lost Leader* (Quartet, 1985)
Gilbert, Michael *Fraudsters* (Constable, 1986)
Grey, Anthony *The Prime Minister was a Spy* (Weidenfeld & Nicolson, 1983)
Stonehouse, John *Death of an Idealist* (W.H. Allen, 1975)
Stonehouse, John *My Trial* (Star Books, 1978)

Chapter 6
Hastings, MacDonald *Mary Celeste* (Michael Joseph, 1972)

Chapter 7
Berlitz, Charles *The Bermuda Triangle* (Souvenir, 1975)
Group, David *The Evidence for the Bermuda Triangle* (Aquarian Press, 1984)
Kusche, Lawrence *The Bermuda Triangle Mystery – Solved* (NEL, 1975)
Winer, Richard *The Devil's Triangle* (Bantam, 1974)

Chapter 8
Berlitz, Charles *Without a Trace* (Panther, 1978)
Berlitz, Charles and Moore, William *The Philadelphia Experiment* (Panther, 1980)

Chapter 9
Babington-Smith, Constance *Amy Johnson* (Collins, 1967)
Barker, Ralph *Great Mysteries of the Air* (Chatto & Windus, 1966)
Garrett, Richard *Flight Into Mystery* (Weidenfeld & Nicolson, 1986)
Goerner, Fred *The Search for Amelia Earhart* (Bodley Head, 1967)
Howard, Ronald *In Search of My Father* (William Kimber, 1981)
Lomax, Judy *Women of the Air* (John Murray, 1986)
McKee, Alexander *Into the Blue* (Souvenir, 1981)
Nesbit, Roy Conyers *Failed to Return* (Patrick Stephens, 1988)

Chapter 10
Bramson, Alan *Master Airman, Donald Bennett* (Airlife Publishing, 1985)

Chapter 11
Breed, Brian *Famous Mysteries of the Sea* (Arthur Barker, 1965)
Gray, Edwin *Few Survived* (Leo Cooper, 1986)
Hardwick, Michael and Mollie *The World's Greatest Sea Mysteries* (Odhams, 1967)
Harris, John *Without Trace* (Eyre Methuen, 1981)
Winer, Richard *The Devil's Triangle 2* (Bantam, 1975)

Chapter 12
Barker, Ralph *Verdict on a Lost Flyer: The Story of Bill Lancaster* (Harrap, 1969)
Tomalin, Nicholas and Hall, Ron *The Strange Voyage of Donald Crowhurst* (Hodder & Stoughton, 1970)

Further Reading

Chapter 13

Christie, Agatha *An Autobiography* (Fontana, 1978)
Oakley, Isobel Cooper *The Count of Saint Germain* (Steinerbooks, 1970)
Pietzner, Carlo *Kasper Hauser, The Child of Europe* (Rudolph Steiner, 1965)